SEEKING AUTHENTICITY

ESSAYS AND STORIES ON VALUES AND TRAVELS

FLINT MITCHELL

Seeking Authenticity
Essays and Stories on Values and Travels
© 2021 by Flint Mitchell

Published by Cowabunga Books in Santa Cruz, CA.
cowabungabookspublishing@gmail.com

ISBN 978-1-7377285-0-4 (paperback)
ISBN 978-1-7377285-1-1 (ebook)

Library of Congress Control Number: 2021918806

All events are personal memories from the author's perspective. Do not use them as an influence to do anything mentioned in this book. The names of some individuals or groups have been changed to respect their privacy.

Cover photograph taken by Matt Montsinger.

First edition.

*In memory of Lieselotte Trautner Mitchell
and Barbara Varenhorst.
The way you spent your time brightened
the world.*

*In dedication to my feet. Sorry for all the abuse,
but we gotta keep moving!*

CONTENTS

INTRODUCTION

Dear Reader,

This book comprises two main components. There are 10 value-based essays and nine travel-based collections of short stories. Because of the denser nature of the essays, I thought that the levity of the stories would provide welcomed pauses. Of course, you can read either the essays or the stories independently—that is your decision.

Concerning the Stories

After leaving my job in 2019, I went on an almost year-long adventure. The trip encompassed the west coast of North America from British Columbia to San Diego, the Islands of Hawaii and Oahu, and the east coast of Australia from Wollongong to Noosa Heads. The main purpose of the journey was simply to spend as much time in the great outdoors as possible, but it ended up being so much more than that. I paddled into unreal surf in waters ranging from 40°F to over 80°F; hiked hundreds of miles across inspiring mountain summits, wide rivers, lush valleys, and stoic beaches; fly-fished in any stream I found suitable for casting; navigated through wonderful, vibrant cities; read dozens of fascinating books; and met a myriad of interesting people.

I am candid and a mostly open book in person; I find great joy in sharing my life with those around me, face-to-face. It seems more meaningful from my perspective. With that said, sharing these stories in a written format feels very private, and I do not take it lightly. These stories are a genuine glimpse of life through my eyes. I intentionally chose to write about moments from my trip that I found particularly funny or meaningful. In transcribing my writings from my physical journals, I elaborated on and edited many of them, adjusting their tone to better reflect my own voice for this format. However, I did not alter any of the actual events. I have been as truthful as my journals and memory would allow.

Concerning the Essays

An inherent truth of life is that it doesn't always go as planned. However, the roots of most suffering can be found in the value system that *you* hold. Your values change your perspective of the world. They tell you what success and failure look like, what you should look like, and how you should carry yourself. But what if the guidance system that you follow is wrong for you? Then all its instructions will be wrong, too. Lead yourself in the right direction by adjusting your character to match your ideal values, and you will aim for the stars and gates of heaven alike.

I believe that you will understand the truth behind the words that follow. The underlying themes of these essays will have this profundity for one main reason: I wrote them solely for me. These values that I lay defenseless before you are my own bedrock, my own moral Vishnu Schist. I have no desire to impress you with my words or impress upon you my beliefs. I only aspire to share them in their most genuine form.

Let it also be clear that I, in no way, claim the creation of these ideas. They were entrusted to me by family, friends, and my wonderful parents; by mental, physical, and literary exploration; by thousands of years of social and biological human advancement;

and by the fundamental essence of our existence, be that God or chance. These values are as real as the matter you breathe. They pull you toward places in life just as gravity keeps your feet on the ground. Though declaring my beliefs about each value is important to me, it in no way touches on their conception. The sun's light was there before you opened your eyes. It will be there as long as you live and will radiate long after you're gone.

I have often heard a clamor of dissent over my use of religious symbolism. I find that religious imagery is often eloquent and easy to understand. Awareness of the idea of God and the heavens is ubiquitous and, therefore, powerful. The actual belief system of any individual should not undermine the meaning behind the imagery itself. If it does, that's your own issue, independent of my writing.

These essays contain a pervasive use of quotations via the experiences and thoughts of others. They may, at a glance, seem an imitation—a cheap trick. Do I stand on their shoulders? Or do I hack at their knees? I hope for the prior and expect review of the latter.

As I recognize the involvement of others, I am mindful of the plethora of quotes I forgot to highlight, books that I lost or that fell lower on my priority list, and words that my ears were inevitably closed to. Alas, I am only human—blunderingly, effortlessly, and perfectly human. These circumstances of humanity have, I believe, made the essays all the more anthropoid in nature. In effect, my inherent human flaws make these essays that much more valuable. We are imperfect beings. It is important to remember that our philosophies are imperfect as well—and that's okay.

These are living documents. I thought as I wrote them that they would be forever incomplete. Written on water, until, over time, they would be contradicted and corrected, not only by others but through my own life experiences—as they should be. Handed off to my reflective mind to ponder until it is time to revisit them. Then they could be written in sand or wood, ever striving for permanence in stone. Those final words, I thought, could only be carved with my last breath. I realize now, however, the flaws in that line of thought. This is not a work in progress.

Instead, each iteration—because there will be iterations—will exist as a completed truth as it is written. This work is finished. It discloses to the world my beliefs on what it means to be a virtuous, good man, which I aspire to be in this moment. In doing so, I shine the sun's great light on any shadows that might conceal my lies or inaction. Will I build on it in the future? Yes. But, when I add to or rewrite it, I will never again be able to capture these thoughts as I do now.

We see wisdom in truth. And what follows is *my* truth. When I look back over these essays, they pull me out of low moments. When my actions lack integrity or responsibility, they reset my mind. When my work ethic or workouts are lacking in motivation, they reset my alarm clock. Many of my friends have told me that they enjoy hearing my thoughts and ideas. With these essays published, I might now respond to them: *You own my thoughts and ideas.* These essays are magnets, which pull me back to my priorities, and now they are yours. Where you let them take you is up to you.

TIME

Only so much do I know, as I have lived. Instantly we know
whose words are loaded with life, and whose not.

— Ralph Waldo Emerson,
The American Scholar

An angel in my life—a remarkable woman whose kindness knew
no bounds—once expressed a poignant thought to me over lunch:
"Time is the most important gift God gives us, and the way people spend it is what separates them from others." How much more
simple could this lesson be? Everyone has a set amount of time,
and that amount is finite. We, as individuals, get the privilege
of spending that time however we so choose, a decision which
dictates the kind of person we become. Some for better, some for
worse. The question, "What kind of person do you want to be?"
would be better stated as, "How will you spend your time?"

Undoubtedly, you have read of many great men and women
in history who took their position in life and did not hesitate to
make the most of it. Marching persistently, they gained experiences to catalyze their future success. They knew that their every
action brought the possibility of great change and would ulti-
mately direct them down their true path. They understood that
the true grace of God is the *privilege of being able to begin*. You get

to begin each morning. You get to begin each new conversation. You get to begin each day's work.

These heroes of history show us that the greatest outlook for living a full life is that of the adventurer's mindset. This is an approach to experience-based living. One that separates an individual from "the mass of men [who] lead lives of quiet desperation,"[1] ever searching for acts that might provide them meaning. He does not remain inside his mind, submerged in contemplation, drowning under the weight of constant speculation. Instead, the prevailing winds of action fill his sails, with only nimble tacks of reflection for redirection.

We've colored the word "adventure" with views of vibrant cities and distant cultures—the rainbows and waves of Hawaii, the Great Pyramid of Giza, and the temples of Machu Picchu. How easily we forget that every day can be an adventure. The verb adventure is defined as, "to risk, or hazard," or "to venture upon ... to dare."[2] Where in this definition does it speak of Himalayan summits or Amazonian rainforests? What bigger risk will you *ever* take than spending your time wisely? You risk losing so many experiences to better yourself, to find love, to find friendship, to find mastery, to find direction. Personally, I define adventure as, "to put yourself in a place where novel experiences can occur."

You might find these experiences by traveling the world, sure. But, you might also find them by building a company, experiencing new cultures in your own city, mastering a skill, building a family, a household, or a community, or by reading a book. The trees have thousands of years of adventures to tell—if only you

---

[1] Henry David Thoreau, *Walden, Or, Life in the Woods* (Boston and New York: Houghton, Mifflin, & Company, 1906), 8.
[2] Various Authors, "Adventure." *Webster's Unabridged Dictionary* (Springfield: C. & G. Merriam Co., 1913).

would stop and listen. If only you would take the time to find out where these stories might lead you. Observe the rich colors of a sunset, try something different at work (be it a new leadership style or simply a smile), or find 30 minutes during lunch to draw or walk or pursue a hobby. You might even sit and watch how the wind moves instead of scrolling through your phone.

It is this search for new experiences that drives a bold life. The hero adventurer does not stay where he is comfortable; he journeys and explores and dares to be great. By foregoing refuge and facing the entropy of the world, he confronts life itself. He challenges the world to give him new experiences that will change him and better him and instruct him. He dips one foot into the unknown where there is excitement and opportunity and the other foot into the known where there is structure and safety. This positions him in such a way that his experiences determine a life which, only upon his death bed, will he realize was the adventure in and of itself.

Had he not first planted himself on the valley floor of Yosemite with a view of its granite palisades, John Muir would have never climbed glaciers and mountains in Alaska. Nor would he have scaled the cascades of the Pacific Northwest or helped preserve the Sierra.

Had she not passionately pursued a connection with David Greybeard and the other chimps of the Kasakela chimpanzee community, Jane Goodall would not have revolutionized our understanding of primates. Her exploration inspired us to reevaluate how we define humanity itself.

Had he not risked his well-being in the bush to save his beloved crocs long before anyone had a clue who he was, Steve Irwin would not have introduced millions to the natural world through his work. He would not have traveled the globe and protected all sorts of animals and environments.

Had she not relentlessly pursued her love of writing and endured the injustices thrust upon her, Toni Morrison would not have found her voice and shaped the literary landscape of America.

Had he not been open to how perceptions can be changed by future scientific observation, Louis Pasteur would not have revolutionized multiple fields of science.

These great explorers challenged life itself. They confronted the world with their actions and demanded experiences in return. As Emerson declares in *The American Scholar*, "the scholar loses no hour which the man lives."[3] Such a man or woman "grudges every opportunity of action passed by, as a loss of power."[4] Pioneers never hide from opportunity; they chase it. Hiding is a sin of omission. It's *choosing* to hinder your growth—to stifle your real, underlying potential. It's *choosing* to be useless. If you hide from yourself and from others, then you are precluding opportunities that *should* have arisen. Mentally, you missed out on new topics, social interactions, and skills. Biologically, you missed out on the stimuli created by new experiences, which in turn change who you are at the neurological level. As time passes, each missed experience inhibits real growth that cannot be reclaimed.

You have a short existence on this earth, and every moment takes you closer to the time when you will leave it. On your last day, the person you became over the years will meet the person that God intended you to become. Can you surprise him? Can you exceed the potential of even God's belief in you? Imagine being on your deathbed and wishing you hadn't spent so much

---

[3] Ralph Waldo Emerson, "The American Scholar," in *Essays* (New York: Charles E. Merrill & Co., 1907), para. 27.
[4] Ralph Waldo Emerson, "The American Scholar," in *Essays* (New York: Charles E. Merrill & Co., 1907), para. 22.

time on YouTube™ or watching the news—that shock alone might kill you.

Wake up every day and risk everything by spending your time wisely—by putting yourself, wherever you are, in the mindset of being ready for your next adventure. Experience the world around you, and let that experience drive your next action.

Realize, too, that these experiences must occur *today*, for all you have is today. Set your aim each morning and then act. Over and over and over again. We tend to want everything *right now*, but it doesn't work that way. There is only living each moment in action and virtue and reflecting on the results. The true wanderer has no aim. The true domestic has no vision. In the middle, we find an efficient medium. He who plans, organizes, and commits—while allowing brief yet consistent periods of reflective freedom and unaided mental exploration—achieves the most direct path toward True North.

Converse with any of your respected elders—or rather, listen to them—and you will see that the path is never linear. Even the surgeon's scalpel may have previously been a paintbrush, inked quill, or calculator, until the fateful moment they allowed their inner witness to take the reins and guide them. But the path to impact as a medical surgeon is extremely arduous, far too difficult for one to simply witness. Once you shift course and set new waypoints and stars to follow, you must now row the oars. With the plan established and your orders commanded, you have only the work left to confront.

This is, understandably, the hardest part. To deliver consistent work means that one must start each day with the right mentality. And I would never presume to have the answer for a lifetime of success in this obligation. However, one thing I know to be true is that every day has a morning, and every morning is a beginning. A designated time for embarking on the adventure of the day, for you will never get anywhere if you don't set off.[5] What habits can we instill at each one of these beginnings? What rituals and patterns can we implement so that we always live presently? Meditation, personal accountability lists, intention setting, journaling, etc. These are all methods developed to put you in a specific state of mind—that which is most receptive to your true desires and value systems. Any method that pleases you will work; rarely is one better than another. Anyone who tells you differently is selling you something. The most important piece is the *timing*. As I have implied, I believe that outstanding days start with outstanding mornings. Begin your days with presence.

Before daybreak lies a time of calm. Nature's dancers are at rest. The winds, unless tempted by a storm, lie at ease. The birds have not yet begun to rustle and sing. The palms don't sway, the grasses don't twitch, the dust settles, and the flowers bow their heads. The potential energy for your day lives in this stillness. It's no coincidence that crime is always at its lowest during these hours. The evening and late night are for those seeking the dark. The early morning is for those seeking the light.

Our mornings are not only times of calm. Productive mornings are a well-crafted, multifaceted diamond. Even unworked and unrefined, their inherent worth is obvious. Yet with expert craftsmanship, each morning becomes a shining object of pride you will carry with you each day. Its glimmer will be seen not upon your hand or breast, but rather in your attentive and reflective eyes. This is a case bolstered by the opportunities each morning brings. Opportunity to reflect upon previous actions, to reorient in a better direction, to begin on projects of passion without

---

[5] Ralph Waldo Emerson, "Spiritual Laws," in *Essays: First Series* (Boston: J. Munroe and Company, 1847).

interruption, to supplement your body with its first nutritious energy. To breathe in crisp air and to begin your day *with* the world, rather than in its wake.

We are programmed to align with the movement of the world, with the rising and falling of the sun, with the cacophony of day and the silence of night. I find this alignment an impeccable determiner for how well I'm living my life. The hours before the sun bestows its yellows and pinks upon the horizon are a time of insight, a time of meditation or prayer, and a time of work. It is *your* time.

Those who feel like the world is slipping from their grasp should heed the early morning. Existing consciously during those daybreak hours may heal your afflictions. Know, too, that it will require sacrifice. Do not awaken dreary-eyed, too tired to appreciate all that it can offer. Go to bed early, and leave the trials of the night to others. You will not regret the trade. You may use any method of accountability for starting your day well, but it seems your greatest chance of success is to apply that method wide awake at dawn. Begin here. Wake up and find a way to engage with the world, and each following hour will build the treasure that is today.

With every morning comes obligations that vie for your attention. Your ability to focus determines whether these responsibilities delight or depress you. What a prize focus is! A necessity for true work and a privilege for the joy it brings. All are familiar with the moments when our periphery dulls, extraneous sounds become silent, and our concentration binds to the moment, establishing attention.[6] This is the beautiful realm where meaningful work finds fulfillment.

---

[6] Charles Johnston, *The Yoga Sutras of Patanjali: "The Book of the Spiritual Man"* (New York: Charles Johnston, 1912), 3:1. "The binding of the perceiving consciousness to a certain region is attention (dharana)."

The result of such focus is twofold. First, the act of focusing intently allows for your mind to let go of distractions. Second, once you've let these disturbances go, true work can begin. Push past that initial barrier of distraction. Your anxiety will clear, your vision will narrow, and your work will pour forth. You can apply this efficient, present, and passionate drive to any endeavor.

We are not measured by the use of our time alone, but also by the impact of it. You only have a finite amount of energy to spend at any given moment; do not squander it by allowing your mind to wander. Concentrate intently on the task at hand. Disregard nonessential ideas and topics, including the outcome of what you are currently doing. Focus on the *process*. Such absorption into a project will bring about enjoyment in your work. Equally as important, it will also yield your best possible results and legitimate pride in what you have accomplished. What better result can be attained?

Herein lies another obstacle. With so many obligations to choose from, how does one decide where to focus? Which issues and opportunities should be prioritized? Obviously, I cannot give a generalization for every possible circumstance. Nor would that even be the least bit helpful. It is more efficient to solve a difficult multiplication problem by understanding and practicing the process than by memorizing a times table. In parallel, I believe an effective method for seeking out opportunities also lies in understanding and practice driven by patience.

Recently, an acquaintance told me that I have a submissive personality. When I opposed this absurd idea, he switched his descriptor of me from submissive to passive. Once again, I refused such a label and instead told him that the word he was searching for was *patient*—not due to my perfection of said quality but due to my efforts toward attaining it.

Where does the line get drawn between the two? When does one shift from passivity to patience?

Being passive is accepting anything that comes your way, regardless of its benefit or lack thereof. It does not involve making choices or accepting responsibility. Passivity is indifference. It is meaningless; it is simply waiting to die.

Patience is also waiting, but of a different kind. It is waiting with *meaning*. It is not seeing a new girl night after night, but rather anticipating a woman whom you believe is remarkable. Furthermore, patience is *active*. It is training every day for a race that is months away or starting to study for your final from day one of the semester. It is getting to work early and being present and focused on your job for however long it takes to get a desired promotion or complete an important deadline. Patience is believing in yourself so resolutely that you are willing to forsake immediate gratification for long-term success. It is seeing that the surf is too big for you to handle and knowing, "Sure, I won't surf these waves today. But in a year or two or three, I'm going to be screaming down the face of that wall of water so quickly, so confidently, smiling so widely, that the time spent waiting and training will have been worth it."

During this period of preparation, you must also be ready to act quickly and decisively—when the time is right. When you think you're ready to surf that wave, when what's holding you back is nerves and not fear, then it is time to check that your leash is strong, that your board is right for the conditions, that you have an entry and an exit plan, and then to paddle out. When a prospective partner's value system, work ethic, interests, and beauty make you stop in your tracks, it is time to share your affections. When you have collected the necessary data and bolstered your conclusions with the truth, it is time to capitalize on your product or publish your work.

Your days define your life. The passive person is invariably at risk of wasting their days and, in a world with infinite stimuli, is consequently at risk of living a wasted life. Such a life omits the necessary use of the word "no." Instead, passivity embodies tentative decisions and weak stances by saying "yes" to everything and everyone.

To spend your time wisely and patiently, you must disregard all that is not a priority to you. You may change your concerns over time through reflection, but your list of priorities at any discrete moment must remain stable. You have work to do—important work. Why would you want to expend energy on frivolous issues or people?

From this argument arises a moral dilemma that is especially apparent in the modern, connected world. This is the harmful conclusion that being a "good" person in the public eye means you must actively combat *all* issues of the world. Pick your battles, and then fight them specifically. Keep your mind open to the opinions of others, of course. If a person or action can convince you that there is a more prominent fight to be fought, so be it. But do not let your arrogance fool you into fighting on every front at once, for it will stretch you thin and preclude your success in any of them.

Dr. Thomas Starzl, the father of transplantation, epitomized such a mindset. His dedication to the exploration of this field of medicine required a courageous amount of patience, which few are capable of. His transplant patients were terminal, and they were unlikely to survive if he failed. For decades he, his teams, and his colleagues toiled. Even in the face of strong opposition to his trials, each success—transplantation of kidneys, groundbreaking immunosuppressant drugs, etc.—provided future doctors with the research and tools to successfully implement transplantation. After a career of effort, his work helped establish our understanding of the process for organ acceptance in a recipient's body. Walking out of the hospital after a study confirming this triumph, he described the "moment of tranquility that followed" as "a fair trade for the 35 years of work preceding it."[7] This was a moment of pride— a moment that he believed would be worth the patient, steady, tough years of labor. He let this experience of accomplishment and joy sink in, "and then it was gone, banished by the next set of questions."[8] Dr. Starzl found a cause worth dedicating his life to, pursued it with all his strength, and was rewarded with the satisfaction of knowing that his work had yielded tremendous positive impact. Had he vacillated from one affair to another, he may have never realized this achievement. And only upon recognition that he had won the battle did he shift his focus to the next undertaking.

To care about a singular or small group of issues does not mean admitting acceptance of other problems in the world. However, to accept *all* problems of the world as your priorities means that you are okay with not changing anything at all. The person who fights one battle their entire life will realize more impact than the one who fights every battle simultaneously. For when they both die, one will have left behind an empire of change, while the other will only have left the reverberation of their voice. What will the world look like in decades if we have infinite jacks and no masters?

In the same vein of choosing the *right* work, you must also choose *how* to achieve it. Technology and science have generated methods for acquiring nearly anything expeditiously. And while this may be efficient and helpful for things like getting groceries or finding job opportunities, it also opens an avenue to counterproductive, self-detrimental, or less meaningful actions. I would pity

---

[7] Thomas E. Starzl, *The Puzzle People: Memoirs of a Transplant Surgeon* (Pittsburgh: University of Pittsburgh Press, 2003), 346.
[8] Starzl, The Puzzle People, 346.

myself if I merely settled for videos of others climbing mountains instead of finding a way to stand on their summits with my own two feet.

Spending your time wisely is not necessarily checking more boxes in less time. That is not to say that efficiency isn't valuable, but I digress. Anyone can skim a book summary, just as anyone can skim through life. The greatest lesson I learned from a mentor and former soccer coach was simple and succinct: "If you're going to do something, do it."

Make a meaningful commitment and stick to it. A six-minute workout every other day will not make you healthy, 100 read-receipt nonresponses are not equivalent to a single eye-to-eye rejection, and skimming the main points of logotherapy is not as valuable as absorbing the entirety of Viktor Frankl's *Man's Search for Meaning*. Such a quick leaf through the pages would mean missing out on the emotions that welled up and blurred my vision upon reading the following in Frankl's book. Here, a prisoner runs into his concentration camp hut, imploring his fellow prisoners to glimpse the incredible sunset:

> One evening, when we were already resting on the floor of our hut, dead tired, soup bowls in hand, a fellow prisoner rushed in and asked us to run out to the assembly grounds and see the wonderful sunset. Standing outside we saw sinister clouds glowing in the west and the whole sky alive with clouds of ever-changing shapes and colors, from blue to blood red ... Then, after minutes of moving silence one prisoner said to another, 'How beautiful the world could be!'[9]

---

[9] Viktor E. Frankl, Harold S. Kushner, and William J. Winslade, *Man's Search for Meaning* (Boston, MA: Beacon Press, 2014), 40.

"*How beautiful the world could be,*" exclaims the prisoner of Auschwitz. *How beautiful the world can be,* I echo, if you *really* experience what is around you and let it sink in and change you. The Nazis stole this prisoner's life and replaced it with the worst that humanity has to offer. Yet somehow, surrounded by atrocity and horror, his captivation with that stunning sunset allowed him to still see beauty in the world. His devotion to that moment is what you must seek in your own life. There are no shortcuts to a better future or a better character. Whatever you believe you should do—*do it.* Sacrifice superficial experiences in life and devote your time instead to that which deserves your attention. Seek out the beauty that will change you.

One example of applying this concept is how much everyone you encounter will appreciate and respect you more if you put distractions aside while conversing with them. An absent parent is an obvious example of neglect. But what of the parent who hides their face in their phone or email during all interactions with their child? Though this parent is not physically absent, the child still may not see the love in their eyes or feel the warmth of their character.

By accepting our own lackluster efforts, we direct our aim toward shallow knowledge. Skimming the thoughts that Thoreau buried in each page of *Walden,* we believe we understand his postures: Live simply! Be responsible for yourself! Do not conform! But this is a crude effort at comprehension. Are these words not hollow, not shallow and empty, without the emotional foundation of the entire text? We have ascribed all meaning to the doctrine of the words, but who is to say that the message is more important than the emotions it provokes? "There is no teaching until the pupil is brought into the same state or principle in which you are."[10] If you abridge and ignore the teacher's words, you impede their ability to teach, and therefore your ability to learn. Aside from the wholly factual—and even in some of those cases—words are useless when not felt. I have learned more from the reaction of my mind and body to most texts than the words on the page alone could have ever offered.

I am deeply affected by the temperament of Emerson, his words constructing part of the trellis that the vines of my mind have wrapped in growth. Yet, "[Emerson] is a thousand books to a thousand persons," if you "take [his essays] into your own two hands and read your eyes out, you will never find what I find."[11] Without personal analysis, letting others influence your interpretation with their opinions and synopses prevents you from establishing your own point of view. Your perspective will always remain hidden because you were too "efficient" to ruminate on the subject yourself. Your mind can't help you understand things you haven't given it the opportunity to know about. And what a sad day it is when a man refuses to know what he might think.

The point here is not that Tinder™ can't find you a wife or that a book summary can't provide you a basic understanding of its main theses. What I instead suggest is that these methods won't make you a better person. If you only care about the surface result, so be it, but if what you desire is a positive change in character, there are no shortcuts.

I once read the mantra, "This life is your choice." Such a statement simply comments on the ability of an individual to make

[10] Ralph Waldo Emerson, "Spiritual Laws" in *Essays: First Series* (Boston: J. Munroe and Company, 1847), 136.
[11] Ralph Waldo Emerson, "Spiritual Laws," in *Essays: First Series* (Boston: J. Munroe and Company, 1847), 136.

what they want of life. It never sounded quite right to me, though. On a long, dark, winter commute, I found it repeating in my mind. Over and over. This life is your choice. This life is your choice. This life is your choice. Until I mixed up the words. *This choice is your life.* It's not that your entire life is your choice— plenty will be out of your control, and it will not go exactly as planned. Rather, every individual choice makes up your existence. Every decision you make and every action you take will define your life. So what actions will you take? How will you spend your time? Will you stagnate and waste it? Or will you choose to spend it wisely and become a better version of yourself?

Know not only the greatness you possess. Understand also the lack of greatness that results from not spending your time well. "Observe the time and fly from evil,"[12] so that you may live! Breathe a life of exploration today, and let today dictate tomorrow. Only in that frame of mind—with a planned yet spontaneous mentality—will you find the adventure you desire. Seek the inspiring sunrise each morning so that all our mornings may gleam brighter. For to "the dull mind, all of nature is leaden," but "to the illuminated mind, the whole world burns and sparkles with light."[13] Let each dawn deliver unto you a strong yet stormless focus. Behold your opportunities with patience. You have more to gain by leaving hollow effort unused and, instead, saving that energy for actions that reflect your values. Act always with the intention of self-betterment and, in turn, find residence in the triumphant world of experience.

---

[12] The Holy Bible, Douay-Rheims 1899 American Edition, Ecclesiasticus 4:23.
[13] Ralph Waldo Emerson, *Journals of Ralph Waldo Emerson Vol. II* (Boston and New York: Houghton Mifflin Company and The Riverside Press Cambridge, 1909), 382.

FREEDOM FOUND

British Columbia and Washington

Hidden in a drawer, underneath some belongings, tucked behind my college diploma in a blue folder, is one of my most prized possessions. Probably not what you'd expect—it's an 8" x 6" folded piece of white laminated paper full of scribbles.

For Christmas in 2016, I asked my parents for a copy of *Freedom Found*, the autobiography of ski and snowboarding filmmaker Warren Miller. I admired the guy. Both of my parents were avid skiers and had told me about his live yearly movies in college, which he filmed, edited, and produced himself. I'd spent quite a bit of time watching his old flicks and even had a couple downloaded on my computer for flights. I always get a kick out of the looks people give me when I start to play *Beyond The Edge* on my stow-away table. The opening scene shows a group of people who wrap duct tape around their hiking boots and ankles, grab some ski poles, and then proceed to "skree"—jumping, flipping, and falling down the loose dirt and rock on the side of a mountain. The action in his films is fun, but it was his humor that always amused me.

I thought it would be interesting to read about the man behind these films. His book gave me far more than I could have imagined. His life was nonstop. Growing up in depression-era Los

17

Angeles with deadbeat parents. Learning to bodysurf before surfing with a board was established on the West Coast. Building his first 100-pound redwood surfboard in woodshop class and then hitching rides to the beach with it before he could drive. Falling in love with skiing. Being shipped out to a subchaser in the Pacific Theater during WWII. Building entrepreneurial ventures to fund his surfing, filming, and skiing habits. Living in a teardrop trailer covered in snow in Sun Valley, Idaho. Starting a filming business that would let him ski around the world. Competing with his son in international sailing events. Pranking the Shah of Iran. Skiing on an active volcano. Being inducted into the U.S. Ski and Snowboard Hall of Fame. He led an incredible life. It's a story of hunger, hard work, travel, of determination to build things better than they were after losing everything, of massive disappointment and tremendous love. It's an *adventure.*

Immediately after finishing the story, my mind was spinning. I didn't necessarily need to do *the things* he did, but I needed to follow my life's path *the way he did it.* That book altered the course of my life back in the right direction, bringing to mind ideas of my childhood heroes—and I wanted to thank him. So, I wrote him a letter, asking some questions and letting him know how much I appreciated his story. As senior year of university wore on, I forgot about it. I did well in my classes, accepted a cool-sounding job, and celebrated the end of my four years with plenty of friends. Everything was going well.

Then, before graduation, I received a letter in the mail addressed from Orcas Island, Washington. I sank to the carpet floor of my room, leaning back against the base of my bed. Eyes already a bit moist, I slid the card out. On the front was a copy of one of his early cartoons. On the inside were some kind words from Warren himself, which ended with, "*Flint ... I wish you success in finding your sense of adventure."* How easily I had forgotten. My dream wasn't only for things to go well; my dream was to live a life of adventure.

From that point on I was always mapping out my next thrill. Starting with small things that pushed my comfort level. Swimming the length of the Golden Gate Bridge without a wetsuit. Trying to summit Mt. Whitney in the middle of winter. Weekend trips all over California. A weeklong camping cruise down the coast in my recently purchased van, gearing up for a much longer journey. And then, finally, with a bed in the back, a cooler and a Coleman grill, a couple surfboards and a holey wetsuit, my camping and fishing gear, half a set of golf clubs, four pairs of boardshorts, two pairs of underwear, and one Band-Aid—I was ready to go.

Where? I wasn't sure to be honest. There isn't consistent surf on the west coast during summer, so I thought I'd head north, toward Canada. Lots of stoic mountains and places to escape.

July 23, 2019

I left home this morning at about 4 a.m. People keep asking me where I'm going but are never satisfied with the answer, "I'm going north ... and then I'm gonna go south." It honestly feels as if I've forgotten everything I've done before now. I have that sensation like I'm getting away with a crime.

July 27, 2019

After several days of traveling, while sitting on a bench in Whistler Village, a ski town in British Columbia, Canada, I was looking out at the mountains across the valley from the resort. Not wanting to continue driving, I asked the guy next to me, "What's the name of that one?" He responded, "Rainbow Mountain." Sounds good to me. The next morning at dawn I started wandering toward it, up the Rainbow Lake trail.

When I got to Rainbow Lake, I sat down under a tree to get some rest. The clouds overhead started to darken and rain. Not too much, but enough. Normally, in this kind of environment, I would be absolutely captivated by my surroundings. A light breeze ran across the lake and swept through the wide surrounding meadow, which was filled with low grasses and blooming wildflowers of purples and whites and yellows. Rainbow Mountain was up to my right, its summit hiding behind a moving veil of hurried silver clouds. But I was too cold and doubtful to be able to take in all the beauty. Though the rain was light, the wind was carrying it sideways into my face. It felt like the first time I had stopped and taken a breath in weeks—or maybe months. One of those "What on earth is going on right now?" moments. I'm 24, unemployed, and all I own is a van and a half dozen surfboards. Though not very far into the wilderness, I was alone in a different country and a bit intimidated by everything.

And at that moment, I realized that was exactly what I wanted. The past couple of years were way too comfortable. I was getting squishy and complacent. I *needed* this discomfort in my life. Without any semblance of a familiar routine, cold and alone, I was forced to ask myself the obvious question: *What do I do now?* I could go on to camp as planned and then try to summit Rainbow in the morning. Or return back to my van and—what? Cry? Drive home and beg for my job and girlfriend back? No thanks.

So I continued on. Finishing the 6 or so miles to Hanging Lake, over the next ridge, I found a place to camp. There was even some good company—a maintenance trail crew, a very chatty Canadian gentleman, and several thousand horse-sized flies.

July 29, 2019

While hiking up Rainbow Mountain, the trail I was on appeared to end. So I decided to wander up to where the glaciated snow covered large slabs of granite. Reaching a relatively impassable point, nowhere near the established route, I sat for a bit. Gazing over the alpine meadows, it looked like the kind of country setting where bears would thrive. I've never seen a grizzly in person, and though there was a sighting nearby two days ago (according to a posted sign from a ranger), it unfortunately appears that I won't have the privilege anytime soon. Turning and looking back over the ridgeline, I could see the valley that held Whistler Village. The feeling of pointing at a mountain you've never seen before and then being in that exact spot 24 hours later is satisfying. Though I didn't summit the mountain, I'm completely content with the trek.

On a less thrilling note, I got a stomach bug at the end of my first week on the road. I'm currently alternating between my van in the Whistler guest parking lot and several café bathrooms. Funny how you can be on top of a mountain one day and then chained to a café toilet the next. I'm not sure if Canadians have ever heard of two-ply.

August 5, 2019

I fell asleep reading *Catch-22* and woke up unbearably cold, in the middle of the night, to the sound of rain. It's lovely when it's dancing on your roof. It's less lovely when there's a waterfall of it pouring through your ceiling fan onto you and your bed. One hell of a wet dream.

August 8, 2019

I'm finally back near the ocean, on the southwest corner of the Olympic Peninsula. Needing to jump in the water, I scrolled the internet and some maps to find a good surf spot near me. Completely by accident, I found what appeared to be the Malibu of Washington: Westport. The surf rolled in knee high, smoke clouded the parking lot, and longboards shaded every car.

I hit up a nearby surf shop to ask a local for information on good places to surf in the Pacific Northwest. When I told the owner that I was from the Bay Area, he made sure to tell me: "This place makes Ocean Beach in San Francisco look tiny. It's not even comparable." Maybe we just get a ruler out and measure our members to see whose waves are bigger that way?

August 10, 2019

On the occasions that I haven't found a good place to park my van for the night, I've been checking out the first-come, first-served campgrounds. After they've already filled up for the day, I'll cruise around, chat up a nice group of people with enough room on their site for my van, and then offer to pay half the normal price to stay for the night. Every single time, they reject my money. After each rejection, however, comes an invitation to park my van for free and even join them for some dinner and a couple beers. "Want a lime with your Corona?" Why yes, yes I do.

Last night at the Crescent Lake Campground on the Olympic Peninsula, I asked these two cute German girls, who were also traveling in their own van, if I could park mine next to theirs. I introduced myself, and we chatted for a while. After having dinner, one of them asked, "By the way, out of everyone in this campground, why did you pick us?" … "Oh, I don't know; it was a roll of the dice, really."

August 12, 2019

My brother wanted to see Vancouver. So I crossed the Puget Sound and drove up to Canada one more time to meet him for the weekend. It was nice to see him, nice to have a heater, nice to use a shower. While hiking in Squamish, we encountered some highliners. They walk on tightropes between cliffs with 1,000-foot drops. I don't have any evidence, but I assume that there must be a negative correlation between the height of a tightrope and the user's IQ.

I've gone on two bike rides with my brother in the past five years. The first one was 56 miles over the coastal mountains of Italy. This time, I followed him 25 miles on a rented road bike around Vancouver, Stanley Park, and the University of British Columbia. Maybe next time we just bike to the park, ya?

August 13, 2019

I drove back across the US-Canada border into the states earlier. The immigration officer asked if I had anything to declare, and forgetting what to or what not to declare, I said, "Uh ... three cans of chicken noodle soup and a half-eaten piece of bread?" Apparently, that's a suspicious answer because it warranted searching my car. In it, they found—wait for it—three cans of chicken noodle soup and a half-eaten piece of bread.

SIMPLICITY

"Pluralitas non est ponenda sine necessitate."
Plurality should not be posited without necessity.

— William of Ockham

Ockham's razor postulates that the simplest possible solution for a given problem is generally the best one. While usually applied to problem-solving and not necessarily an absolute, I extrapolate its meaning to be profound in many facets of life. The best way to maneuver the content of our days—from our calendars to our speech to our art—is most likely the simplest one. Our world presents the possibility for so much complexity. And in some respects, it seems like we are conditioned to embrace it without question. But for the most part, it is overwhelming.

The modern man must, in parallel, manage a vast network of peers; dozens of different forms of entertainment; his daily addictions; as well as his many civic, work, and personal commitments. Through this busy and convoluted lens, it is no surprise that we are being overpowered in our everyday lives. And while we cannot eliminate certain aspects of our lives, such as work, there *are* ways to lighten their burden. Sometimes the most beautiful art is that which does not embellish. Sometimes the most articulate speech is silence, and the preferred presence is absence. Sometimes the greatest way forward is simple.

The first step during times of stress or trouble is to simplify. Clean up parts of your life that aren't serving you. A month without alcohol, drugs, sugar, caffeine, pornography, TV, staying up late, bad friends—or whichever vice calls to you—helps create clarity of mind. The main benefit of this is that, with time away from potentially harmful voices or vices, you gain an objective view of how it has been impacting you. By observing both the positive and negative consequences of this action, you can decide impartially whether it still deserves a place in your life. And if you conclude that it does, you can then consider healthier ways of introducing it back into your world.

Certain patterns and elements of my life still astound me when I realize their uninterrupted involvement in my day-to-day—for example, a year or two of drinking alcohol basically every week or indulging in caffeine nearly every single day. Intentional breaks from these stimuli are breaths of great knowledge and self-learning. They help build a realization of how your habitual actions are impacting your well-being.

I have found through personal experience that taking a break from or eliminating vices makes it much harder to converse with certain people. These may even be close companions or family members. Self-restraint can often compel others to project their own noise onto you. They might say your vice isn't harmful, and that might be true. But you must learn for yourself what is best for you.

Know that if you feel like something is wrong in your life, the validity of that feeling is not dependent on the other person agreeing with you. It is *your* responsibility—not theirs—to take control of your life. It is up to you to determine what is dragging you down and decide if you will stand up against it or not.

Those friends might be scared that your new actions will reflect poorly on them. Or that your change somehow makes you a different person. They might fear you're driving a wedge in the relationship, creating distance, or pulling back. Perhaps your growth turns up the volume of their internal voices, even if just for a moment, causing them discomfort. Or maybe they have invented a self-centered reality in which your goal is not self-betterment, but a personal attack against them. What they don't comprehend is the potential of simplicity. The control you can attain through the deliberate choices that you make in this life.

In this same vein, there is no adequate reason to force your changes onto other people. Live your own life. It is not "worth [your] while to be solemn, and denounce with bitterness flesh-eating or wine-drinking, the use of tobacco, or opium, or tea, or silk, or gold."[14] There is no time for one to scorn his old ways or the people who still participate in them, nor to act as if his growth merits any extra attention. One may still appreciate the extravagance of a grand theater or respect the penchant for wine without partaking. Be proud of yourself because of your decisions, not spiteful about those who don't wish to join you.

Eliminating vices in your life creates a space that might feel empty or difficult to sit with. This feeling seems counterintuitive—was that not the very intention for getting rid of them in the first place? To create room for new actions and events and people? The dilemma here is that when you create a void in your life, you must then fill it with something. And to change how we spend our time is to change, even momentarily, who we are. There are big moments in life—entry into college or a new job

---

[14] Ralph Waldo Emerson, "Heroism," in *Essays: First Series* (Boston: J. Munroe and Company, 1847), 6-7.

or a cross-country move—where some will relish this opportunity to start anew. However, it can also be an anxiety-riddled experience.

At first, you may find that these new actions and habits are harder than those of your old routine. Additionally, your closest friends might not want to join you. Your life will likely become more difficult. Why would you do this to yourself? Why would you consciously remove from your life things that were allowing it to run smoothly, even if they weren't bringing you success or joy? Because you decided that those habits, views, actions, and relationships were squandering your life. And you knew it. And you still know it. *And you will always know it.*

Room for new actions and habits is but one of many places where a lack of simplicity brings resistance. In my introductory years studying engineering and working in a scientific field, I found frustration and an extreme resistance to men who convolute their speech. My conclusion is that the intelligence and observable confidence of a man is greatly related to the simplicity of his language. When we're insecure, we find a compulsion to deflect with cryptic words. This is an effort, even if a subconscious one, to obscure the message being conveyed. Further interrogation on the subject of interest will only yield an array of complex explanations and jargon. Those who hide this way have tied their identity to the difficulty others have in understanding their work because it makes them feel good. Note that I do not intend to dismiss the work of such individuals, only the attitude in which they speak of it. It is obvious to discern he who talks for another and he who talks for himself.

Of course, specific vocabulary is necessary when immersing yourself in a field of expertise. You must define each aspect in order to understand it. But I believe that the fact of the matter remains:

There are very few terms too complex to be explained with an example, an experiment, or simpler words. This simplification might not give you a complete understanding, but it will give you a basic one, encouraging further exploration if you so choose.

Reminiscing on his early adolescence, Benjamin Franklin understood this to be true in his debates with an older, more educated friend. "He was naturally more eloquent, had a ready plenty of words; and sometimes, as I thought, bore me down more with his fluency than by the strength of his reasons."[15] Someone who acts this way, as if his speech cannot be simplified, is trying to fool you, either into thinking that he is smarter than he is or that his field is more difficult than it is. These must be the same people who believe that a longer job title corresponds to more responsibility or talent. If you are worth your salt, the content of your work speaks for itself—without unnecessary exaggeration.

Always be wary of a man who refuses to simplify his words. The smartest men speak so that anyone may learn. They do not hide behind the veil of big words. They do not intentionally make conclusions that a passerby might not understand. On the contrary! They make an effort to be accessible. For they want you to understand and appreciate the cleverness of their work!

I want you to know what I know! It is only then that I might realize the errors in my logic and in my ways. It is only when you know what is in my head that we can come together and build upon an agreed base of knowledge. Because we feel most connected to those details that are the easiest to interpret.

While in Rome years back, standing under the *Creation of Adam* with my brother, I was quite moved by God's image. Though

[15] Benjamin Franklin, *The Autobiography of Benjamin Franklin* (New York: P. F. Collier & Son Company, 1909), 17.

the painting may be surreal, his face is recognizable, familiar even. It is not his grandeur that is the most affecting, but his simple humanness. That he looks like a man, whom I could understand. One who would speak straightforwardly to me of his life. Of the things he finds important and of the things he deems beautiful. All because his eyes and his expression are honest. Not altered or embellished, but real and simple.

WHERE THE WIND TAKES YOU

Oregon

August 16, 2019

The forecast predicted the first decent swell of the trip. Nothing too big, which was good because I hadn't surfed in a while, and I was excited to spend some time in the water. I found a cool, pretty well-known beach break in Northern Oregon. A magnificent place to surf. There is a big bluff on the north side of the cove that protects it from the north winds, great tide pools to wander around and watch the dinner-sized dungeness crab look for food, and beautiful rock arches in the water. In these environments, you get to experience the bounty of life that the ocean ecosystem provides for.

Small crabs and snails crawl across every inch of sand, clams bury themselves, and shorebirds point their beaks at any movement that might be a meal. The rocks are densely covered in mussels and barnacles. Each tide pool is a great collection of light purple-orange starfish, jade green anemone, and swift little fish hiding in refuge from the tides and the predators that they bring.

My first day surfing, the waves were still waist high and the water was around 63°- 64°F. This surprised me because that's even warmer than the ocean in the Bay Area at almost any time of the year. However, I soon learned that the winds up here bring with them rapid swings in water temperature. Consistent north winds can bring the temperature down by about three or four degrees in a day. By the third day I paddled out, the swell had gotten larger, with waves breaking overhead,[16] and the water was 48°- 50°F. Not a great situation, wearing my 4/3 mm neoprene wetsuit, barely held together at the seams where I had stitched and glued it the month before.

The next day, I waited to go out until late afternoon's low tide, when the previous day's waves had seemed to be the best. At this point my arms were pretty tired, having not paddled much for a couple months, and I was both freezing and not finding much success. Right before deciding to head in, the guy 20 yards to my left pointed to the end of the bluff. A larger swell started to break over a previously hidden, deeper reef. A heavy set of green-gray waves was rolling in. I scraped for the outside, where I would be safe, but couldn't make it before they started to break. The power of the first wave caught me off guard while I tried to duck dive it, a method for pushing the board (and myself) under the oncoming foamy whitewater. The explosion from the lip of the wave crashing too close to my head ripped my board from my hands and quickly introduced me to the seafloor. Since rock outcroppings

---

[16] One of the most common and consistent methods for measuring the size of waves is to use a person standing at its base as a reference. "Waist high" would mean about 3 feet from the base to crest; "head high," 5'–6'; "overhead," 6'+; "double-overhead," 10'–12'+; etc. This issue opens up a can of worms—wave height in the world of surfing is a rather subjective issue. Do you measure the wave looking at it from shore or from the surfer's perspective, behind the wave? A 6' wave in California might be labeled 3' in Hawaii, simply because of the higher levels of testosterone. Overhead for Shaquille O'Neal would be four times-overhead for a golden retriever (I've seen it). The only thing that is clear to me is that at the end of the day, no one really cares. For the purpose of this book, however, I'm 5'9" (for the ladies reading this book, disregard that, I'm 5'11"), so that will be the approximate measurement of a head-high wave.

lined the floor, I felt lucky to only encounter sand. More of a skin exfoliation than a cheese-grating.

After maybe five seconds, the wave released me to the surface, where I was greeted, less violently, by the remaining five waves of the set. The current then pulled me sideways into a slight riptide. By the time I had gotten back on my board, I was already three-fourths of the way out to sea again. At this point I was exhausted, my teeth were chattering, the sun was going down behind the overcast gray clouds, and I was a bit spooked. Shivering, I paddled inside and bodyboarded a wave back to shore. Fortunately, there were no more mysto sets[17] on my way in. Solid end to the first swell of the trip.

August 17, 2019

While in Westport, WA, I was asking around for surf breaks further south at my next destination. Surfers are secretive with good waves, especially up north where there's still a lot of apparently hidden surf. No videos, pictures of secret waves flipped so rights look like lefts, names bleeped out in interviews and magazines, etc. No one wants their secret wave to turn into the next Malibu, with hundreds of people crowding to it. So when this guy looks on either side of him to make sure no one is listening, then leans over and starts whispering to me, I'm pretty sure I'm about to find a really cool place.

I get to the spot, and it's as Oregon as I could possibly imagine. There's a set of dirt trails that lead from the parking lot for half

---

[17] Mysterious sets of waves, larger than most of the others that day, which break further out in deeper water and roll through where everyone is currently sitting on their board. Also known as a "cleanup set" for its ability to clean up a group of surfers. Exemplified by the set mentioned in this story.

a mile through a tall, dark green forest out to an incredible white, sandy beach with clear blue water. Both sides of the cove are stoic rock cliffs covered in patches of forest. And what else? *Easily* 200 people surfing. I think your secret's out, bud.

August 18, 2019

Patrolling Google maps, I saw a big peninsula called Cape Lookout. There was a northwest swell coming in at an angle that I thought might wrap around and break at its point. I parked and started hiking the two steep miles down to the beach. I met a guy on the trail who was walking up with a board and asked him about the surf. He said, "It's alright, a couple good shoulders[18] to ride!" But when I got down to the bottom, there were no rideable waves. I don't know why, but it's still wild to me that the surf at two beaches a mile (or less) away from each other can be completely different because of the shape of the coast. North of the peninsula, the ocean was in chaos, covered in white caps from the gusty wind with unorganized and unruly well-overhead waves battering the beach. But south of it? It was 80 degrees in the sun with no wind and no waves. Resenting the idea of climbing back up immediately, I made the responsible decision to put it off by taking a nap.

August 19, 2019

Hiking north of Lincoln City, on a popular trail called Cascade Head, I met an older couple just before the top. As we talked, they asked about my trip and then reminisced about their own travels at my age, in which they spent a year wandering through Latin

---

[18] The corner of a wave, which breaks slowly enough for a person to catch and ride it parallel to the beach.

America. After roaming from Venezuela to Guatemala, there were two things that stuck with them. First, as is almost always an answer for travelers, was the difference in cultures. The different pace of the rural towns and the compassion of their residents. Second, which I hadn't heard before, nor really appreciated until now, was that it provided a period of time to think without too much interruption. At a young age, they took a full year to live a unique experience—creating art and music and exploring other cultures.

I grew up in the Bay Area, a place that is losing its personality. Cavalier tech marauders are quickly outnumbering the locals. Where your worth as a human is generally associated with the estimation of your potential IPO valuation. Or that your company's name rhymes with "oogle," ends in "book," or is inspired by a certain fruit that might keep the doctor away. That's the environment I was raised in and the type of person I was becoming as a young adult. An electrical engineering student who got a job in a scientific field, looking toward graduate school or trying to start a company, mostly for lack of having other perceivable ambitions. I appreciated hearing from this couple that taking an unconventional path, even if for a brief period of time, paved the way for a more deliberate direction in their lives. Upon saying goodbye, the man left me with one last comment: "You should try and let your creative mind take over for a bit. Build something you'll remember from this time in your life."

August 21, 2019

I saw a guy coming out of the Yachats River mouth with a surfboard. The wave looks fun but comes with some dangers. Namely, the dark brown-green water, the obvious rocks, the groups of harbor seals, and the eerie feeling that I'm being watched by a big fish with big teeth. Maybe next time.

In Yachats, I gave a hitch to a nice Hawaiian guy I met. He was also traveling south—with a tent, a surfboard strapped to his back, and his thumb out. While we were talking about places we had surfed on our travels, I mentioned one spot where I didn't get into the water because of the aggressive locals. I found it while sitting on the wall of a vista point, probably 750 feet up. When I looked down between my feet, I saw an awesome right-hand point break with only three guys out, peeling for a while around the side of the cliff.

Meandering my way down through the neighborhood to get as close as I could, I parked right as a guy was walking off a trail from the beach with a surfboard. I asked him about the point break, and he kindly responded, "Yeah, it's great. And no, you won't be welcomed if you go out." After this warmhearted response, I went to go look at it—one eye over the dunes, one eye on my new friend who was noticeably interested in my van.

When I was caught eyeing the waves from the shore, I received some fairly unaffectionate looks from the guys in the lineup. Deciding against it—because I'm alone, and if they screw with my car, they're screwing with my home for the foreseeable future—I moved on. The Hawaiian guy laughed at this story, and then said that he was actually there that same day. His friend was helping him out with a ride from Washington into Central Oregon. They paddled out, and his friend got in a fist fight with one of the locals, who then keyed their car. I took that as confirmation that I made the correct decision.

August 23, 2019

"Hi, is this the Bandon Dunes Golf Pro Shop?… Do you have any cheaper rounds? Maybe a twilight round to play 18 holes? … No? … $300 for 18? … Yeah, no, I think I'll be alright … okay, thanks. Yeah, have a nice day."

August 25, 2019

Southern Oregon is a beautiful emerald stretch of coastline. There are tons of peninsulas jutting out into the sea with large rock formations. Emblematic of the Pacific Northwest in my opinion. After the sky seemed like it would never let up being overcast, the warm sun shone through. Newly blue skies contrasted with the lightened color of the water, which changed from the more stormy intense grays to a pleasant jade blue-green.

I went for a surf near a creek inlet south of Port Orford. It looked so nice that I forgot my neoprene gloves and hood, which was a mistake because the water ended up being just over 40°F. I spent almost an entire hour after surfing laying on the hood of my car trying to bake myself back to a livable temperature.

While thawing out, I met two guys who came to check the waves. The swell here, protected from the north by the Port Orford Heads State Park, was small, in the chest-high range, and the guys were debating whether to surf. While they were deciding, I reminisced on my own drive down the coast this morning looking for waves. The first spot I checked out was further north, near Bastendorf Beach, where the waves were bigger. But there was no chance I was paddling out there alone due to the stormy conditions and the hundreds of seals at the point nearby. The general rule of thumb is: If there are healthy seals in the area, there are also healthy sharks. As the barks and grunts of the seals resonated in my mind, one of the guys pulled me back into the present by saying to his friend, "Oh come on man, Bastendorf will be bigger though. You're just scared because you got nudged by a great white out there. You're getting soft." Let the scoreboard read, Flint: 1; great whites: 0.

August 27, 2019

When I'm in the ocean, my mind tends to wander to the mountains. When I'm in the mountains, my mind tends to wander to the ocean. I drove inland to spend a week or two exploring the cascades. Earlier, as I was walking on a ridge near the top of Mt. Scott, one of the small peaks surrounding Crater Lake, a hawk stopped me dead in my tracks. The northwest winds ramped up the west side of the mountain, gusting over the ridgeline and under the hawk's wings. The hawk hovered on a pinpoint in the air, 20 feet in front of and above me, its body perfectly still, every muscle silent—even the tips of its feathers appeared motionless. For maybe three minutes the hawk stayed there. And for those three minutes I stayed as still as it was, my knees bent to hold my balance against the strong winds, not wanting the moment to end. The clouds moved quickly across the sky, my disheveled hair whipped in front of my eyes, my skin vacillated between being warm from the sun and cold from the wind, the trees swayed. But we were still.

Then, without warning, it twitched its head left and then right. It pinched one of its wings in slightly, dove 10 feet closer to the ground and closer to me, released its wings wide, sailed straight up, and then floated south effortlessly on the current of the wind. I stood and watched it fly for a minute or two. As my eyes drifted from the bird down to the horizon, they locked onto one of the great wonders of my home state, over a hundred miles away. Mount Shasta. *I'm on my way.*

HEALTH

The one thing in the world, of value, is the active soul.
This every man is entitled to;
this every man contains within him,
although in almost all men obstructed and as yet unborn.

— Ralph Waldo Emerson,
The American Scholar

Your health is of the utmost importance: Your body and mind deserve quality sleep that nurtures and rejuvenates, healthy food and water that nourish and sustain, physical activity that strengthens and stretches, and a joyful attitude that allows you to flourish and completely embrace life. There should always be a healthy desire to live in a body that can physically take you where you need to go. As important as the physical is the psychological, for mental fortitude is what creates the opportunity to build a successful life. With such toughness, you can take on emotions and challenges, stay calm, and then act objectively. Fear will no longer cause anxiety or hesitation, but instead foster an environment of growth and opportunity. You have caught a glimpse of your potential. You have seen what lies on the other side and will do everything in your control to not let poor health stand in your way.

We all have a vision of the ideal version of ourselves. Dreams of our ideal self encompass these "perfect standards," not only in how we act, but also in how we feel and look. Appreciating beauty at the fundamental level is not superficial. Only when your physical image becomes the priority has your appreciation gone too far. We go astray into such frivolous affairs with the misunderstanding that beauty is only bound to looks.

Such is but one hue of your portrait. The look of real health is not only physical; it is difficult to portray in a simple image or magazine cover. Health may have power and endurance. Yet, "raw steel unadorned causes unease, [while] steel joined with flowers is another matter."[19] Health combines flexibility, peace of mind, and strength. It has an efficient cardiovascular system and a solid mind. We know health when we see it, but it is not just because of the image that our eyes perceive.

Healthy people exude a palpable energy. When you look at images of Duke Kahanamoku, Mia Hamm, Laird Hamilton, Serena Williams, or David Goggins, you don't just see their strength—you feel it. They are physically strong, but also *vitally* strong, exuding that mysterious power or attraction of life itself. These are men and women who have endured adversity, external or internal, and faced life's challenges with vigor. It is almost tangible when they walk into a crowded room, all eyes immediately cast toward them with regard. Look in the mirror and feel your health. Understand that your image and the energy it gives off are a good reflection of your well-being.

Emerson depicts heroic stories as the ideal actions taken by others in the past, in which we see the potential for ourselves to achieve.[20]

---

[19] Thomas E. Starzl, *The Puzzle People: Memoirs of a Transplant Surgeon* (Pittsburgh: University of Pittsburgh Press, 2003), 15.

[20] Ralph Waldo Emerson, "History," in *Essays: First Series* (Boston: J. Munroe and Company, 1847), 6. "So all that is said of the wise man by Stoic, or oriental or modern essayist, describes to each reader his own idea, describes his unattained but attainable self."

The men and women who inspire merely by their presence—by the perfection of their posture, the light in their eyes or the calmness of their psyche—are the physical ideals of health that we see in ourselves. We do not simply want to *look* like our physical ideal, we want to *feel* how they do. Your cells, your very fundamental genetics, have that potential in them, if only your mind would allow you to make such a transformation.

I have yet to meet a man on a high mountain trail who watches to make sure that he doesn't overeat for fear of gaining weight. He cares first about the structure and purpose of his body before ever even noticing the shape. He seeks functional strength and elemental knowledge. With this said, have you noticed that those who drive at the apex of life *tend* to *look* the part? It is as if their intention to live a powerful, hard-working, healthy life manifests the physique and energy that eludes so many.

The vice grip of a trained heart pumps oxygenated blood into every corner of our bodies. Pushing into every recess of our souls, feeding us the energy needed to climb mountains and cross any finish line. Each beat of the heart resounding, much as the organ shakes the steeple. Let it be felt by your closest companions, not just from ear to chest but across valleys and nations as well. Robust lungs draw out calm composure and firm will, that we may navigate any adventure. Each breath acts as the wind in our sails, like a profound gale across the oceans.

Plant your feet firmly in the ground. Dig your toes into the dirt, turf, or sand, so that the strength of your stance would even leave impressions in rock. Then stand proud and show your own spirit the great potential you have through this energy. Take a deep, gratifying breath and hold it inside with control. Soften your eyes and drop your shoulders back. Release the breath and pronounce, "The energy of this stance, of my upright posture, of my calm self, of my eyes clear and my heart ablaze, of my lungs full, of my feet steady, of my ears open, is what true human vitality conveys. This is the energy of efficiency, of fitness, of pride in my body and mind. This is the energy that tenaciously and resolutely ascends the high mountain summits of my life." *That* is health. It is not two plates on a barbell, a three-hour marathon, a 100-foot freedive, nor a stack of trophies or medals from prior races. Health is the embodiment of that proud energy constantly exuding from your soul. Exercise is merely one tool used to access it.

This energy is a balance between the physical and the mental. The way our body feels, as well as how we use it in labor and in movement, deeply affects our psychological state. In efforts that thoroughly push my limits, my body and mind become both exhausted and joyful. I have found it common to experience these states of being simultaneously. Thirty miles of hiking has brought me a broader smile than nearly any other success. It is evident that the occasional experience of *complete* exhaustion is connected to my mental health. I might go as far as to say that a man who has never felt this fatigue has never lived. You may find it in a marathon run or a marathon of work, but welcome and embrace encounters with your limits.

This connection is a double-edged sword. The body can be treated with exercise, sleep, and nutrition, which all will help build a healthier psyche. But a strong body cannot compel the mind to be healthy by itself. There are demands which the spirit must resolve independently. One of the most challenging is the ability to rejoice while encountering any emotion. The trained, resilient mind is one that accepts its surroundings as reality and does not shy away from them.[21] When you can embrace each state of

---

[21] David Goggins, *Can't Hurt Me: Master Your Mind and Defy the Odds* (Lioncrest Publishing, 2018). This is not a direct citation, but I believe this sentiment is a main thesis of David Goggins' book.

physical being and every emotion directly. When you can accept them all in whichever form they come. When you can let them pass through you without harm. Then you start to become solid—capable of accepting negative experiences in life with vulnerability while continuing to pursue your ambitions in their presence.

Adopting this ethos allows you to engage any challenge without fear. You will take each opportunity, no matter how extreme or farfetched, and dissect it impartially, carving away each layer, each "how can I ... ?", until you have found the most probable route to success. Even if insurmountable, you will have determined its impossibility through analysis, leaving you confident, as opposed to avoiding it due to shock, leaving you too timid to make an attempt.

These challenges might come in the form of a physical experience, such as a race, test, or sickness. They are just as commonly manifested as emotions. It is my perception that resilient men and women understand that each emotion they encounter, ranging from euphoria to despair, is equally important. After graduating from university, I wrote the following to a woman, which I still find to be relevant and true:

> *Upon moving to a new city far from friends, with a long commute, doing work I had never done with people I didn't know, I discovered a variety of feelings. Some good—pride, independence, joy—and some bad—nervousness, loneliness, fear of the unknown (both for myself and my future). However, I realized during introspection—after reading The Book of Joy and When Breath Becomes Air—that these are nothing but signs of vitality. To feel is to be alive. Yes, to be joyful or proud is to be alive; but to be nervous, afraid, or sad signifies life as well. Those who restrain and suffocate their emotions are merely restraining and suffocating their*

own lives. This helped me understand that even when I have intense feelings that gnaw at my energy and happiness, leaving me a total nervous wreck, it's merely a sign of life. It's a sign that trillions of electrical potentials are ricocheting around the neurons in my head ... that my heart is beating ... that I can continue learning no matter where I am ... and most importantly, that I am alive.

A solid man knows he is alive. He knows that every encounter with depression is as important to his humanity as every encounter with joy. He knows that, when he confronts sadness, it will pass—if he does not fight it. His anguish, his fear, "even his despair ... is an existential distress," and an opportunity for growth, "but by no means [is] a mental disease."[22] There is nothing wrong with him for feeling that way.

Such episodes are superficial fractures in bone. Live in acceptance of sorrow when sorrow comes knocking, and the body will heal these fissures stronger than ever before. Avoid sorrow, and your wounds will never mend, leaving vulnerability where there should be steel.

One specific emotion, which I find to be of paramount importance to our health, is fear. Fear is a compelling phenomenon. It can make you do things you didn't expect. It can halt you in your tracks, causing anxiety, depression, guilt, or pain. However, if treated and addressed appropriately, it can also lead to pride, joy, confidence, and a myriad of other beneficial emotions. Just as it can cap your potential, it can show you that many of the pinnacles that you originally thought were out of reach are very much attainable. Though fear may bring opportunity, know that hesitation lurks in its shadow.

---

[22] Viktor E. Frankl, Harold S. Kushner, and William J. Winslade, *Man's Search for Meaning* (Boston, MA: Beacon Press, 2014), 102.

Hesitation *can* allow for valuable, momentary thought. But hesitate a moment too long, and you may end up frozen, with a higher risk of getting hurt. This may occur physically by getting knocked over by a wave, monetarily by not doing well in a job interview or negotiation, personally by failing to attract a desired partner, professionally by failing to close a deal, or emotionally by not saying words that needed to be said.

Hesitation causes the greatest failures of all—those "what if … " moments. It leaves space on the table for something more. You may always wonder what could have happened, how you might have filled that space. But, if you put it all out there—if you leap instead of stalling—there will be no need for "what if … " You gave it your all, and you can only learn and grow, whatever the outcome.

Many of our failures in life come from the subconsciously created loop built by hesitancy and fear. A positive relationship with fear allows the mind to analyze results that they do not want to happen. A negative relationship with "fear brings about that which one is afraid of, and that hyperintention makes impossible what one wishes."[23] You are afraid that if you talk to her, you will be awkward. You are afraid that if you don't get to sleep right now, you will be tired tomorrow. You are afraid that if you don't do well in the interview, you won't get the job. You are afraid that if you can't get an erection or orgasm, you won't be able to satisfy your partner.[24] And now look at you, you're awkward, exhausted, jobless, and impotent all *because* you froze in fear of those outcomes.

---

[23] Viktor E. Frankl, Harold S. Kushner, and William J. Winslade, *Man's Search for Meaning* (Boston, MA: Beacon Press, 2014), 125.

[24] Viktor E. Frankl, Harold S. Kushner, and William J. Winslade, *Man's Search for Meaning* (Boston, MA: Beacon Press, 2014), 122.

Of those things only should one be afraid
Which have the power of doing others harm;
Of the rest, no; because they are not fearful.[25]

There will always be environments or actions that bring out nerves and fear. If you let them control you, if you are afraid of everything, then you have deceived yourself into a fictional reality where you are incapable of growth. Where you will exhibit weakness and hesitation for the rest of your life because you are too scared. Seek out that which draws fear into your eyes. Not for personal endangerment, but to find the line between where you are safe and comfortable and where you are nervous and afraid. For that is where you are in the most optimal environment for progress. Succeed in this trial of fear and find the excitement driven from standing toe-to-toe with yourself, demanding commitment.

This is where moments of extreme presence and wonder lie. These moments draw emotion and inspiration.

Imagine yourself floating in the ocean with a friend, the blue-green water gleaming around you, the heat from the bright sun balancing the cold of the water. A tiny, fluffy, newly born otter lies several body-lengths away. It's squeaking loudly while its mother is diving for clams, then squeaking even louder when it hears her surface and chirp to him. Brown pelicans plunge their long beaks below in search of a meal. The kelp beds pull briefly under the surface as small swells roll through, disrupting the glassy texture of the water. You notice your friend smiling while watching the scene with joy, and you find you are grinning as well—no words need to be expressed for such emotion.

---

[25] Dante Alighieri, *The Divine Comedy of Dante Alighieri,* Translated by Henry Wadsworth Longfellow (Boston: Ticknor and Fields, 1867), Volume 1 (Inferno), Canto II, Lines 88-90.

Then, off in the distance, larger swells of water appear, traveling swiftly, bending left and then right as they reflect off the contours of the ocean floor, quickly approaching and converging near where you sit. The current has pulled you slightly out of place, so you move toward them a couple strokes, then inside, where you know they will peak and break. They've been coming in sets of six or seven this afternoon, and you see the waves in the back appear to have a bit more height to them. So you pause and paddle over the first and then the second and then the third and then the fourth, when suddenly, right in front of you, you are greeted by what appears to be a mountain of water.

It's about fifteen seconds off, and it enthusiastically says, "Hello!" After all, it's traveled thousands of miles across the Pacific, and it's clearly happy to see someone. You're not sure if you've ever seen anything so magnificent and find yourself in awe as you paddle closer. Eight seconds off, now seeing your intentions, it says a little more hesitantly, "Are you sure?" Your heart beats a bit faster; thoughts of pulling out race through your head. But by the time it is two seconds from you, you've already turned toward the shore, and those thoughts are nonexistent. All that exists are the few moments ahead of you. You're jamming your arms down as deep as they can go under your board, pulling yourself forward with as much purpose as you have, each strong kick propelling you. Its voice is muffled slightly by the spray of the feathering top of the wave, which has also momentarily blinded you. But still you hear the wave speak clear as day: "Alright ... then get fuckin' ready."

You rise vertically, already almost a story above where you were a moment ago, and then you're on your feet. And you're falling—wait, no. You're flying. In a second or two, the drop forces you into a squat as you turn off the bottom of the wave, knees crouched, with both hands in front of your face pointing toward safety. All your weight is

centered over the front side of your board, which is turning and slic-
ing through the wave, clearly bending under the pressure.

Some of the potential energy this wave created by picking you
up has turned into kinetic energy in the form of you speeding
down the side of it. It feels like your guts have dropped down
into your thighs and your heart into your stomach. Your friend
is 75 yards away, turned around after the wave he caught, and
he's watching everything. There was too much potential energy to
start, however, and while most of it fueled your speed, some of it
instead became chemical and spiritual energy—a double shot of
epinephrine straight to your soul. Maybe this is what the Hawaiians felt as "mana." Your friend's hands are both raised to the sky,
and he doesn't even consciously know it. You're screaming down
the side of the wave. Not just physically with speed—you are literally yelling out loud. And your friend is yelling. And the couple
on the cliff watching is yelling. And the otters are yelling. Screw it,
maybe even God is yelling, "CHHHYYEEEEWWWW!!!" Wel-
come to "stoke."

Primal grunts like this are not desires for attention; they are
the externalization of overflowing stoke—an unbridled, almost
otherworldly, energy. The adrenaline from that wave might wear
off, but the smile that ensues will last for a week. Like a balloon
being filled with too much air, when there is no more room left to
contain it, it bursts. The first yodel must have been yelped before
anyone knew it would echo or herd livestock. That first yodeler
had no choice but to let out a rapturous howl in excitement, perhaps while taking in the view from a summit. Only then would
he discover its reverberations off of the alpine peaks and ridges.
Same goes with the vociferations of warriors through time: that
of the Māori dance known as the Haka, the Roman battle cry of
"Barritus," the Navy Seals' "Hooyah." Perhaps, they later realized

such shouting could inflict intimidation. But these calls were most likely the result of an energy felt by a single person or collectively by a kindred group that could no longer be contained. They had no choice but to grunt, hoot, whoop, and yell.

To be clear, it has nothing to do with surfing. I have found these shouts to be more prominent in my own life as I have grown more consistent in my actions. At more reasonable places like concerts and award venues, sure, but also in less common circumstances such as seeing friends or while watching intense sunsets. My understanding of this progression is that as I grow as a person, I am able to see my own potential for a more fulfilling life, and the excitement from that manifests itself with shouting toward the sky.

From this, I have concluded that part of being healthy requires self-love in the form of being able to see yourself as worthy of success. Why is it easier for people who are fit to stay fit? It's not just that they feel the benefits; it's that they have already seen what is possible. A huge topic, it appears to me, in the "self-help" world is this ability to recognize that *you are worth being better than you are.* People who can't do so, whether subconsciously or consciously, will never put in the work required to unleash their body's potential. They will never build the solid mind of the mentally healthy. You must believe that a greater potential is attainable if you are to ever attain it. If you cannot see that vision, then you must create it. The judgement lies in *your* eyes.

You determine your fate. Not only that: You also determine your body fat percentage, VO2 max, breath rate, heart rate, and posture. You determine your work ethic, quality of partner and friend group, and what time you go to sleep. You determine the trajectory of your life, the good you will do in this world, and the joy and love that you will feel. And it all starts with your ability to *see* what you are worth. Before cutting, a surgeon must believe that they are, in fact, capable of doing the surgery. Their endless studying will be useless and harmful if they do not believe that they can translate that knowledge into action. Likewise, endless thought and cycles through the world of self-help will be futile if you do not believe yourself worth helping.

This is a critical topic because it creates a visual awareness loop. When you see yourself as worthy of success, you strengthen your abilities by working harder and focusing better. In return, you believe in yourself and your capabilities even more. Better work delivers better results. After achieving better results, your vision widens, and it sees that your potential is even greater! This positive feedback loop is only possible if you can see that it is possible.

People had been actively pursuing the four-minute mile for over half a century by the time it was broken. Soon after being broken, many others followed. Today in 2021, it is a common performance among professional runners. This does not trivialize the unbelievable amount of training needed to travel at a rate of 22 feet per second for four minutes—an undoubtedly extraordinary feat. But it does show the impasse was mental and not physical. Once four minutes was achieved, others saw its possibility in flesh and blood. More importantly, they saw its possibility *in their own flesh and blood.* And they rose to the occasion. This may sound optional: *choosing* to see a better you and then *choosing* to better yourself. But, really, you cannot avoid it. You are *always* in the loop, for better or worse.

The inability to see a better form of yourself inherently means that, right now, you see yourself only as capable of your current state—or worse. Perception is the precedent of action, and if you don't see yourself as capable of exceeding your current state, then you will act in a way that leads to the deterioration of your life.

When your life gets worse, you may see this as your new normal, and, consequently, spiral downward. Henceforth, your vision is something you *must* pay attention to. Stagnation will not lead to a better life. View yourself with positive potential, or face the risk of squandering a life of possibility.

You are not alone, however, for there are eyes all around. I must preface this by declaring that others can never decide the status of your health—that privilege is reserved for you (and your doctor). But your vision is inherently limited, and you can only process so many things at a time, let alone from so many points of view. So if you have a goal in mind or a value that you wish to uphold, then it may prove beneficial to ask those around you for honest input. Simple inquiries such as, "How am I doing with … ?" or "Do you think I could … ?" can give you invaluable external insight.

Confidence in yourself is an important character trait, but it should not obviate accepting help from and connecting with others. External observation can be a constructive secondary assessment. Take in this information objectively and with appreciation, even if it hurts initially. Granted, they simply may not be able to understand your real efforts. Or … maybe you aren't working as hard as you thought you were. What are you going to do about it? Will you ignore their advice and keep believing your own story? Or are you willing to see if there is any truth in their words that might conflict with your own beliefs?

Our vision is limited, and that can be a blessing. We constantly sort through thousands of stimuli, but can only pay attention to several at any moment. This means that we are *all* actively ignoring the majority of what surrounds us *at all times.* Understanding that our perceptions are not all-encompassing is a wonderful opportunity to embrace the world around us with intentional concentration. Whether life is going as planned or not, there is *always* more to see, experience, and know. With this principle, you can push yourself to learn. All you must do is stop and shift your attention toward something that was originally out of focus.

You have this ability—this superpower—at your fingertips. How do you plan on using it? Will you choose to open your eyes to the world around you? Will you choose to view the world as full of opportunity? Will you visualize a better life for yourself? More importantly, will you visualize a better version of yourself? What does that better version look like, what does he speak like, what kind of presence does she bring, what do they value?

Envision your life with clarity. Recognize that the unity of a strong body and mind is not just a matter of health, but also the embodiment of the self-reliant soul. He who prides himself on his fitness and rejoices in his mental freedom will know what it means to be independent. Every punch he throws and every word he declares will be bolstered by this trust in himself. He can take on challenge after challenge with trust in his complete being. With the groundwork set and with his structure solid, all his actions will possess the weight of his entire character.

The man who takes responsibility for his health appreciates that the power to control his actions, his body, and his mind comes from inside—from the power of a vigorous soul. Know that the pride of your heroes, your idols, and your gods is within you. Each action they took, each decision they made, each abstinence they enjoyed, you may also manifest. See them not as your final aspirations, but instead as mere cobbles on the promenade toward the solid constitution that is your life.

UNDER A DARK REDWOOD CANOPY

Northern California

August 29, 2019

Warm wind curled around the rock, keeping me comfortable as I rested on the giant granite slabs after my morning hike. The sun started to take its afternoon stroll across the sky. As the light crested over the wall, my body began to re-energize for the second time today. I let my hat slide off from over my face and my eyes flickered a bit, adjusting to the near-direct rays from above. Sitting up against the wall, I kept my torso in the shade, as the sun crept over my feet. In front of me, a vulture slowly ascended from the dark green forest floor several thousand feet below. Each time he circled, he climbed, soaring to my eye level within 10 minutes without a single flap of his wings.

There is a great harmony in this picture. As the morning sun warms the great stone palisades of Castle Crags, they in turn radiate this heat out into the nearby air, compelling it to rise. Then a vulture, whom I imagine flies here day after day, as familiar with this particular thermal as he is with good places to sleep, comes to play in the warm current. The sun emanates heat down to the earth and the life it touches uses that heat to spring upward. The plants grow and the birds soar.

Shuffling a bit to the side, I peered over my right shoulder. The sky was pure blue—for if there is a real definition of blue, it is certainly the cerulean mountain sky. Without any clouds, the only visible white came from the glaciers on top of Shasta. I tracked with my eyes where I had slowly ambled up her side the day before. Up Green Butte Ridge on an iffy scree ridgeline. I stood upon this very spot months before as well, when it was blanketed in snow. Though it looks quite treacherous whether frozen or not, the loose rock is a far greater deterrent than the snow for hiking further up. Standing on that ridge yesterday, I looked toward exactly where I rested next to Castle Dome. Only in the mountains can you travel real distance by eyesight.

If the sun were to stay still, then I would too. But it does not, and so I mustn't either. As I meandered back down the crags to my home on wheels, I saw my slender, scaled, orange-pink friend, whom I passed earlier on the way up. He moved off the path once more for me, rattling goodbye. I told him not to worry; I will be back soon.

August 30, 2019

Near the town of Shasta, I walked out into a couple of pools and bends of the Sacramento River to see if I could find some fish. I forgot to bring my fly-fishing waders or boots on this trip, so I've been wandering out into rivers in my board shorts and wetsuit booties. I'll admit—it's an eclectic look. Fly-fishers are a great group of people, but are usually quite consistent in their attire and serious about their gear. Seeing this jolly kid, smiling and laughing to himself, in neoprene booties and half-neon board shorts sloshing around their rivers with a fly rod generally compels them to walk the other direction. All good, we can't all be this cool; it might scare the fish away.

After catching a series of 6" river monsters, I wondered why I couldn't coerce anything larger to bite. And while I can't make any conclusions, I have a suspicion it might have had something to do with the group of homeless people I saw frolicking and bathing around in the water upstream afterward. Actually, homeless isn't the right term; they have a great camp set up right on the river. Cheapest waterfront property in California you'll ever find.

September 5, 2019

At around four this morning, I drove up into Redwood National Park. With a hot cup of coffee, I sat on the hood of my van off to the side of the narrow road, watching the night in silence as the stars cascaded across the sky in the still air. Followed by a guttural trembling of the earth as an occasional logging truck with high beams passed by, several feet away.

Disregarding the intermittent trucks, the early morning whisked my mind back to college. After diving further into my studies, I found great peace in the mornings. When interested in a project or wanting to understand the material for the next test, I would wake up around 4 a.m. and go to the library. With a pourover coffee in hand—I love those couple of zen moments watching the steam rise as you pour hot water over the grounds—I would drive out of my apartment complex, past my favorite taco shop and bakery, over the rail line and highway, and arrive at campus.

Sliding into a table in the newly built main hall of our library, I'd reach into my pocket and pull out a pair of earplugs. Earplugs already have the great effect of blocking out the noise around you. But in the stillness of the morning, they have an extra, almost magical feel. Transporting you to a place where all that exists is what's in front of you. Outside this scope of extreme focus it seems like there is no light, nor sound, nor stimulus of any kind.

And it would stay that way until the sun came up and dreary-eyed students would start filing into the library to rest their heads on their books. As my mind drifted, a pair of stars roared across the sky above me and brought me back to reality. I left the warm memory of the past behind for the cold forest air of the present.

September 6, 2019

At Prairie Creek Redwoods State Park this afternoon, I asked a ranger about a trail out to the beach and back. He informed me that it's about 12 miles, but that it was too late to start today. "The old growth redwood forest canopy is so dense that it starts to get dark early—and once it's dark, *it's really dark*." Of course, suggestions from park rangers only apply to the average, obese American, and most definitely not to me.

With this thought, I started off toward the coast. A bit over three hours later, far before when I thought it would get dark (and exactly when the ranger told me it would get dark), with somewhere under three miles left, I was walking back on a different trail, completely alone, in a very, very dark forest. Darkness, much like the coldness of the Pacific, is always less scary when you are prepared for it. Though I had a headlamp, my ego prevented me from being more mentally ready for the near-complete darkness. When you're not fully expecting it, it's always a bit more alarming.

September 12, 2019

"Fin!" "Dude, shut up, that's a rock … oh … never mind." There were quite a few people out surfing on this beautiful sunny afternoon. But probably 300 yards down the beach from where I sat, people started paddling in. Past the ones getting out of the water, the fin patrolling the coast became pretty obvious, even that far off in the distance. Out of curiosity, I asked a paddleboarder who had passed near the shark if he could identify it. He told me he thought it was a salmon shark, about six feet in length. Salmon sharks are relatives of great whites and have similar coloration and build; from afar, they can easily be mistaken for each other. Regardless, it didn't appear to be coming up to anyone in the water or showing any aggressive behavior, so I didn't think much of it.

As it swam closer to my side of the beach, people near me started filing out. The now empty lineup meant more open waves, so a couple of us stayed in. My logical mind knows that the chances of being attacked by a shark are slim. But your logical mind is quick to change its tune when you're processing the smile of a great white shark. Especially when it's swimming toward you an arms-length away, and you're on a five-foot, nine-inch piece of styrofoam, with all your limbs floating in the water. It's in these moments that your mind doesn't tell you things like, "Oh, chill out man, sharks aren't indiscriminate killers, and it knows you aren't food. It's clearly just coming over to say hello and ask why everyone is getting out of the water!" Instead, it says things like, "Is the risk worth it for a couple shitty waves?" and "You're an idiot, aren't you?"

We'll call that a tie game. Flint: 1; great whites: 1. Not a game I feel compelled to keep playing.

Time is
Too Slow for those who Wait
Too Swift for those who Fear
Too Long for those who Grieve
Too Short for those who Rejoice
But for those who Love
Time is not.

— Henry Van Dyke, "Time Is"

CONNECTION

The world's perspective turns and changes hue,
But there at the end will always be you.

Words of fire scorch the golden land ablaze,
Nourishing the soil for future days;
Sowing seeds where a Sequoia might grow,
Root to canopy, a strong, lasting show.

The stars fall, they streak across, and they shoot,
But never from the sky will they uproot.

Edged rock caressed by storms alone,
Eroded dull still preaches solid stone.
Leaves fall, rain drops, flowers spring, seasons dial,
Return though each morning the warm earth's smile.

Salt blonded hair blown to gray and then gone,
Yet forever your eyes relent love's song.

Such simple shows of Nature abiding,
Represent here our internal guiding.
For the buried bedrock of our heart's desire
Never fractures, not now nor past the pyre.

Scornful seas will twist, will taunt, will torment,
But even open oceans repose beneath the sun's ascent.
We progress, falter, go high and then low,
I see now, that this is all I know:

The world's perspective turns and changes hue,
But there at the end will always be you.[26]

— "A September Wedding"

---

[26] A wedding present I gave to a best friend, written under a late summer sunset in the Santa Cruz Mountains.

Every person you connect with will change the worth of your character. Whether your life gleams or tarnishes at the end will partly depend on the people you have chosen to let into your life. It is the great aim of our relationships to create strong, genuine bonds. Ones that not only influence each person positively, but allow for true, mutual expression. By doing so we are able to fully appreciate some of life's privileges that are only found in connection. Through a helping hand, a compassionate ear, or our innate affection for those we cherish, we experience the full expanse of human emotion.

To be yourself—especially the finest version of yourself—is to create an atmosphere filled with people that will embrace it. That means choosing your location, peers, partners, mentors, and colleagues wisely, if possible. "A man's growth is seen in the successive choirs of his friends. For every friend whom he loses for truth, he gains a better."[27] Deliberately choosing your loved ones is hard. It requires culling people in your life that do not bring the best out in you and then letting them go. Though difficult, know it true that the actions and attitudes of our peers have a real influence on our own. Surround yourself with well-intentioned men and women, and you will find the level of your character always rising. Surround yourself with fools, and you brazenly pledge yourself to be a fool as well!

Selecting people who might be a positive influence on you is but the tip of the iceberg, for relationships are reciprocal. Once chosen, it then becomes your burden to act in a way that merits their worth. This means building up a personal independence that

---

[27] Ralph Waldo Emerson, "Circles," in *Essays: First Series* (Boston: J. Munroe and Company, 1847), 279.

does not drag them down. When you act in a way that makes yourself proud, it will make others proud to be around you.

No discussion of external connection, however, can begin without first directing your attention internally. This can be exemplified by two commonly abused personality traits. The classification of extrovert and introvert is a jail, and I have never understood the compulsion to imprison oneself within it. I do not necessarily deny the existence of such groups; I simply reject the esteemed worth of their use. They are examples of cursory limitations we establish in our minds and of biases we welcome into our perception. If I were to give in to the description of an introvert, my mind would urge me to avoid gatherings of potential friends and family, and a poor man I would become. If I were to give in to the description of an extrovert, I would then at all costs avert opportunities of solitude. I would lose touch with my own self, and an equally poor man I would become.

You may suggest that a person who knows if they are an introvert or an extrovert can use this information to grow. If you are aware that you are uncomfortable in group settings, you can actively attend them in order to get out of your "comfort zone." The issue with this train of thought is that you have already declared yourself uncomfortable before placing yourself in the setting. You have thrown out the opportunity to embrace the experience as novel and therefore preclude yourself from entering with an open mind. You are already uneasy because you told yourself you should be. Even stating "I will be comfortable" to oneself beforehand is simply the internal proof that you believe you will not be.

Similarly, if I am to tell myself that I will feel lonely when I am alone, I may forgo exciting solo opportunities based on the assumption that to be alone is always to be uncomfortable. I do concede that I've found myself quite proficient at never, or rather very rarely, being lonely. The most common protests I have heard in favor of not being alone regard safety, companionship, and enjoyment.

On the matter of security, being alone *can* put you in precarious situations. However, it can also bring out and foster a healthy relationship for our primal, yet apparently lost, intuition. Your safety is not based on your environment alone but is also a factor of this primal awareness. Even if placed in a hazardous, yet inevitable, situation, you are at greatest risk when you lose touch with your instincts. Listen to this internal sensation if found entering an environment with the capacity to harm you. Being conscious of potentially dangerous circumstances is the first step toward taking yourself out of them. Friends are secondary to your intuition when it comes to safeguards.

As for companionship, in a world quickly approaching eight billion people, there are only a few areas left—which are quickly and unfortunately going extinct—where you can be legitimately disconnected. If you do not feel as though you have recently enjoyed engaging conversation, it is not because it is hard to find. It is because you haven't honestly tried. Go to any café, park, beach, library, museum, theater, market, bar, downtown, uptown, or any other place with people. Arm yourself with a genuine smile and sense of curiosity. Raise your pedantic view, look others in the eyes, let go of your expectations, and open your ears. Friendship will arrive.

The stories you will experience may surprise you. I have heard tales of battles in the Vietnam War and lessons learned from them, met elderly women who worked in some of the first computer science labs in the world, and listened to whispered secrets of hidden hikes and waterfalls. All because I sat with a cup of coffee and wore a face of sincere interest.

Lastly, enjoyment should never be dependent upon others. Exist so that you may resound with these words of the independent Thoreau: "My life itself was become my amusement and never ceased to be novel."[28] Too often, I encounter people who refuse to do something that excites them for lack of a companion. They don't think that they can have fun on their own. What a duplicitous belief. Life must be lived before it can be shared! You choose to sulk by refusing to try something enjoyable because it *might* be more fun with another person. Certainly it could—often a loved one enhances an experience. But should not having them there at all take away any experience that is to be had? If you wait to live your life until another person comes along, you will never live it at all.

Most importantly, these objections of solitude do not broach the main issue, which is the topic of personal companionship. Your best possible companion stares back at you each day in the mirror. Not only *can* you be your own greatest ally, *you must be.* You lose yourself when you tend only to the presence of others. Being alone is a physical state; being lonely is a state of spiritual loss. Much as the agnosia patient has lost the ability to perceive stimuli, the lonely man has lost perception of his spirit.

I prompted this passage, however, by relinquishing that I am very rarely, not never, lonely. It's apparent that one catalyst for loneliness is the relatively immediate displacement of people or other stimuli with solitude and silence. I imagine that when I am surrounded by my friends celebrating the union of lovers or the

---

[28] Henry David Thoreau, *Walden, Or, Life in the Woods* (Boston and New York: Houghton, Mifflin, & Company, 1906), 125.

reunion of family, my spirit lingers after I am physically gone. Dawdling, dragging its feet, not wanting to depart. How can I blame it? It is in these times that I am lonely. It is in these times that I crave not to be alone. For this, the only cure is patience.

Be kind to your kindred spirit; it thrives on love. Let it soak up every moment of embrace with your loved ones or with the crowds you have recently withdrawn from. This does not have to take place in person. A memory with enough emotional energy—a reminiscence of rapture—can dislocate your spirit from the present. I've experienced this with smells, songs, and sunsets. For this again, the only cure is compassionate patience. You will again soon be whole.

The simple act of being alone should never be a driver for loneliness. Embrace your time of solitude, whether it occurs in a tent, in a forest, swimming in the Pacific, climbing in the Sierra, at night or during the day, at dinner, or in bed. If you are lonely during these moments of solitude, it is because you have chosen to be. You have severed yourself from your spirit, and it waits for you to restore contact. Establishing this personal connection and independence is the foundation for interaction with the outside world.

The benefit that independence grants to relationships is exemplified by the matter of control. It appears that those who have true sovereignty over themselves do not feel it necessary to command over others, simply for the sake of doing so. The independent see support, not control, as the answer. For support emboldens others to be strong. Will you reach out with an open hand? With curiosity and compassion? Or will a desire for influence shroud your words of assistance?

In the past, I have tried to fix my partner's problems. I have offered unwanted advice. I have responded to friends in trying times with my ears closed. In these situations I, even without the intent of malice, have attempted to exert my control over my companions. I only now know of my error. I know now that even if I meant to protect, my results may have been harmful. Harmful to the relationships and inherently harmful to my partner. For by exerting control over someone, that person will instinctively put up a barrier. You wanted them to let you in, not push you away, correct? Furthermore, by preventing the person you love from struggling at all and always trying to protect them from the world, you obstruct their path toward building personal strength. And it must be even harder for them, if while they are trying to grow and get stronger, their partner is trying to take the opportunity to do so away from them. So, they not only fight against what is pushing them, but also against the person who should be supporting them.

Do not confuse support for control. The difference lies in their origins. Whether vocalized or not, the desire for support can only be conceived by he who needs or wants it. Once a stranger, friend, or partner acknowledges this conception, support can be openly given. Control, however, is born in the mind of the passerby. Let others figure out where and when they need support. Not only does this foster healthy connections, it fosters an environment of independence. Would you rather your partner love you freely or love you out of necessity?

Selfish flattery is another carelessly negative action that is far too common. When you compliment someone, the praise should be for the *other person alone*. This may sound straightforward, but ask yourself to reflect on the last compliment you gave. Did you expect anything in return? Even a "thank you"? If so, I dare say that you gave the adulation for yourself. Most will see through this act.

A compliment is a genuine expression of compassion, given for no other purpose than to show appreciation for an attractive, impressive, or otherwise redeemable trait, quality, or performance. In no part of this definition does it mention the objective of a trade or a request for anything in return. You would do better talking about the weather than giving such selfish offerings. For one should never feel indebted when receiving admiration. Furthermore, if I was to receive utter silence after giving a true compliment, or if that person were to even insult me afterward, I would feel no embarrassment. Nor would I have any regret for the esteem that I paid. For in my mind, at that moment, what I said was true. To try and take it back would be a lie.

Before ever praising a person with words, can you first admire them without? Appreciate them with your ears by listening. Applaud them with your gaze by paying attention. Did you tell her she had beautiful eyes in a feeble attempt at getting her phone number? Or did you tell her because her eyes stopped you and took the wind from your breath? Be her admirer, not her beggar.

It should be no surprise that this topic is pervaded with commentary on the ability to listen. A helping hand without open ears holds a tyrant's decree, not broken bread. Listening is a prerequisite for creating strong connections. Not only that, it is also essential for the ability to think analytically. I define analytical thinking as *listening* to yourself without attempting to validate your own beliefs. That proficiency in listening can determine your ability to connect with others *and* to think critically is a testament to its importance.

It has become almost cliché to say that one of the hardest things we can do is see the world from another person's perspective. This saying is common because so many have decided to be deaf. They read something, having already determined what has been written. They hear someone, having already determined what has been said. They see actions, having already determined why they were carried out. What they will never comprehend is their *incapability* to understand others. These are people that respond before the other person has finished speaking. And no man—absolutely no man—is capable of responding well to something without actually thinking about what the other person has said. Let them finish speaking first. What narcissism is this that plagues the human mind? If you do not listen to your companion, why even converse with him? In all responses, I know if a person has listened or if they have chosen to try and shackle me in their own perfunctory opinion.

Attentive listeners deliver more to a conversation than themselves. They start by bringing their surface level identity—their current wants and desires. Then, they unearth deliberate thoughts and meditations. Each person takes the information given by the other and then spends time developing ideas on the subject before responding. If there are no pauses in your discourse whatsoever, it is because you do not think before speaking. Those who believe a pause in a debate declares them as victor have arrogantly deprived themselves of both the opportunity to understand and to connect. They will be stuck in their own ways because they refuse to let others take their time to think. What does it matter that a response takes a moment? I'd rather my companion return a conscious thought the following day than promptly give me their thoughtless drivel.

Know, too, that listening is not just a skill for connecting with those you love, but also one for supporting them. By not listening, you inhibit your companions' potential goodwill from positively impacting our world. The unwitting attempt to deprive others of their speech by oppression with your own is a delivery mechanism of evil. If you rob your adversary's ability to speak publicly, you prevent their ideas from being heard. The prejudiced will produce their own downfall if allowed to speak openly. And if you concurrently deprive your friends' opportunities to speak, you prevent their opinions from accompanying your own in the face of injustice. By not listening, you enable your enemies and annoy your allies.

Every conversation is a bridge between two people with many opportunities to cross it. But you may not traverse it without listening. Seek out those questions, statements, and claims that thirst for further commentary. The ones that show true curiosity. Each one of these comments is a chance to delve deeper and connect more fully. It is not enough to know that your friend believes certain things. In order to connect with him, it is imperative you seek out *why* he believes them. Only then can you understand who he is as a person. Only at that point will you be able to open up to the same degree and forge a friendship of understanding. Listen so that you may learn. Listen so that you may better yourself. Listen so that you may connect. Listen so that you may speak.

As the ears open and the mind processes, there is a moment of creation where we find the opportunity to unearth empathy. The primary reason this is important is because it establishes an emotional link between two people. If I try to empathize with you, it is not that I am trying to feel your pain, it is that I am trying to care about you. I am offering a hand for you to grab hold of. I cannot assume that I will ever *actually* know what you are going through, nor can I assume everything you say to be fact. That is of little relevance.

The purpose of empathy is to connect us. Only after establishing this connection can we try to solve the issues that afflict us. We might subsequently converse about your or my or the world's problems and share perspectives. After connecting on an emotional level, we can then switch to an analytical mindset. Because it is true that if you open yourself up without any analysis, you are destined some day to be fooled. You might then wonder why this initial step is necessary. Why not skip it and go straight to objectivity? The answer is because without the bond created by empathy, you may find it hard to take seriously those who differ from you. When conversing, start with an effort to make a strong emotional connection, *especially* when it comes to those you disagree with. Do this, and you bring love into your heart for them. From there, you may more respectfully and thoughtfully discuss the trials of tomorrow.

Unfortunately, empathy has been cheapened and stands currently as little more than a buzzword in job applications. Instead of an ethos to be lived, it has become a show. Celebrated by the world of self-help. A box to check toward becoming a great leader. A façade for selling to a larger audience. A performance to put on, whether or not you genuinely reach across the aisle. I concede that empathy may help build the foundation of many grandeurs. But the classes, seminars, and cults that try to teach empathy to you, in reality, deceive you. In exchange for your money and time, they provide you foolish arrogance. The feeling that you understand without true understanding. You do not learn empathy from another; *it comes from within.* Those who proclaim empathetic excellence preach to you like the common man talks about the surface of the moon. Regurgitating descriptions of pictures and videos that they have seen but have never, and will never, experience firsthand. For your experiences with empathy—your bonds with others—are always unique. I could never teach you how to love your brother or sister, only you can do that.

When you feel for another, you relate your own independent experience with theirs. This opens the doorway for empathy, but it is not enough. Once the doorway is opened, you must walk through it. You create a link by tying a rope between the other person's experience and yours, but now you must walk that rope. Let go of your own experience and assume their perspective. Without this crucial piece, you simply feel bad for the other person. That's just pity. By attempting to see their situation from their own eyes, you endeavor to feel as they do. And while no one can re-create exactly how another feels, to try *is* enough. What is important is the emotional bridge that you establish, which only you and they may cross.

Empathy is a complex feeling where the real component is the physical situation, and the imaginary component is the emotional response. If we focus only on the physical, we lose the emotional. Without both, it is impossible to fully characterize the connection and observe the entire picture. This lack of desire to see the emotional component of the equation is emblematic of the walls that humans have put up between each other. We shield ourselves too much from the soul of our brother. Do not look at his life—at his living quarters or his clothes or his status. If you wish to know about a man, look into his eyes.

Why is it so difficult to give anyone—friend, family, or stranger—such recognition? Is it because we do not wish to know about the other? Or is it because we do not wish for them to know about us? Of course! The reciprocal empathy! Build a bridge between you and another, and they might cross it into your soul as well. Yes, as with all relational interactions, empathy is a two-way road. It is only real when the mind, with all its anxieties and uncertainties, shows its cards to another.

But what does the man find who patiently puts in the work to connect with someone else? Simple. By being sovereign over his own mind, he gains the ability to give himself wholly to his relationships. When he finds someone he respects and cherishes, his actions are not aimed at controlling them, but instead at intertwining his own independent life with theirs. He finds in this space a compelling force which pulls not at his body but at his spirit, as it, in turn, pulls at his kindred's spirit. He no longer listens to the simple words of his companion, but instead seeks the meaning behind them, focusing on their intonation—their being, their wants, their fears, and their desires. Just as dry bushes and shrubs accumulate beneath a forest, attentive listening, selfless embraces, and each moment of his endearment bolster companionship. Then his intimate acts of empathy and compassion provide the spark and oxygen to set that tinder aflame. And it is here, enkindled and blazing with passion, where he finds the conflagration called love.

Love is a many faceted element of our lives. Much like fear, it can make us do things and feel ways we never expected. And that only makes sense. What else could follow in the wake of the questions it brings? Questions like: "Will this woman be a lifelong friend? … My one partner? … Will he be the godfather of my children? … Will we travel together? … Summit mountains together? … Will he speak at my wedding? … Will they speak at my funeral?" Love brings with it the nervous realization that you will let this person see *all* of you. You are willing to consistently let them in. Allowing them to see the best and the worst of you and everything in-between. Know that they feel the same nerves—what a tremendous embrace that is. I could not think of a more human experience!

> *No man ever forgot the visitations of that power to his heart and brain, which created all things anew; which was the dawn in him of music, poetry and art; which made the face of nature radiant with purple light, the morning and the night varied enchantments; when a single tone of one voice could make the heart bound and the most trivial circumstance associated with one form is put in the amber of memory.*[29]

---

[29] Ralph Waldo Emerson, "Love," in *Essays: First Series* (Boston: J. Munroe and Company, 1847), 158.

Here, Emerson speaks of adulation, but there are, of course, many types of love. Love between partners and family members. Between friends, owners and their pets, even between strangers who find a common ground. There is no need to catalogue each type, however. It is only important to understand that these different types of love exist. For "no one can become fully aware of the very essence of another human being unless he loves him."[30] It is not about the type of love, but rather that you *have* love in your life.

So build yourself into someone who lives a life you're proud to share with others. One that is capable of entrusting your core to another. One who ties himself securely into the network of mankind through real, positive relationships. Find that your own independence will bring out the same in others. Listen and learn from the intrinsic values in others, which might complement your own. Maybe we will connect in a way that allows each person the opportunity to bring their best self to the light. Maybe we will live in a world overflowing with connections embodied by love.

---

[30] Viktor E. Frankl, Harold S. Kushner, and William J. Winslade, *Man's Search for Meaning* (Boston, MA: Beacon Press, 2014), 111.

SURFING ABOVE THE STARS

Santa Cruz

October 4, 2019

I called the caretaker at the hospice center where I was volunteering before I left. I meant to do it a couple weeks ago, when I passed through home, but I got caught up and forgot. The patient who I've been spending time with has her 100th birthday in a week! I was so excited to celebrate it with her. But she died. Last week. To be fair, she lived far longer than the doctors told her she would. "They keep telling me my heart isn't working, but I'm still here, aren't I?" I'm sure she was counting down the days until she hit triple digits. On the other hand, I don't think she cared. She was happy to wake up and smile every day.

It would have been nice to see her one more time and to tell her about my trip so far. She was so excited for me when I was building my van, always wanting to see pictures and hear about my adventures. I'm not sad about her death, just reserved. I'm glad I was able to bring her some joy during her last year. It was the least I could do for all the joy she brought me.

October 13, 2019

The tide was rising slowly, and with it, the waist-high surf was getting a bit mushy and inconstant. Nothing too great, but perfect for a relaxed longboarding session before bed. Though it was a beautiful Sunday in Santa Cruz, it was also pretty quiet. There were only a handful of people still in the water as I paddled out, uncommon for this usually crowded area.

As I surfed, each wave was a different experience; the world gleamed in the respective colors of the sunset. Paddling back from my first wave, with the sun starting to touch the ocean, the light was nearly blinding. Ten minutes later, the cliffs warmed in the red-orange glow of the sky. Then as the orange started to fade to twilight, the water, without almost any movement from the offshore wind, radiated a greenish pink. Like that of a new rose bursting from its bud.

My last ride that night, however, was something different. It was not just a different hue, but a different sensation. The light all but left for the night and where the darkness of the sky met the darkness of the ocean, the horizon disappeared. The others had gone back to shore, and I was alone. Only the glare of the moon and a purple tinge from the end of twilight remained as I bobbed up and down on the dark surface.

One last rideable wave emerged, seen only through glints of reflected light converging on me. As the ocean swell picked me up and my board started to glide, I walked several steps up. Not all the way to the nose but enough to feel the water spraying off the rail as it trimmed through. My right hand hovered at shoulder height over the curl of the wave as I cruised down the line, standing with both feet together, a slight, comfortable bend in my lower back, left hand resting at my side.

Without daylight, the wave itself was not really visible. Not in the usual sense. The moon reflected off the wave's dark face but was not a still circle—it was a superimposed stream of light on a deep purple-black background. The ocean now existed only as an image of the stars in the night sky with an infinitely long shutter speed. Streaks of white and beige-yellow flowed beneath me. Silver veins that bridged the skies to the shore. It was as if I was riding on a current of light. Each bump on the face of the wave a small ripple in space. Ten seconds of enchantment that slowed down time itself. And then, as I slowly faded off the shoulder, the light I rode waned and weaved away, seemingly back toward the ocean. Maybe toward the horizon to jump up and rejoin its family above. Kneeling on the board, I paused and gave the Pacific one last look. My other sensations started to come back—hearing the crashing shore break, smelling salt in the air, chilled from the water. Looking ... waiting ... but the lights were gone. I turned and headed back for land.

Those are the moments I've been searching for on this trip—and in life, I suppose. Experiences that make room for themselves in my mind. The wave itself was mediocre at best, especially if encountered in the daylight. And yet the experience of riding it ... I will feel that within me always.

October 14, 2019

I just watched someone burn[31] another guy at The Hook, a crowded right point break (as if that description needs to be given for a surf break in Santa Cruz). As the fugitive paddled back into the lineup of surfers, I was kind of hoping to see a fight, but all I got was a loud flaccid dick-measuring competition: "You think you local brah?? I local 25 years, you fucka!!" ... Reminds me

---

[31] To burn someone means to paddle into and take a wave when the other guy was clearly already in and riding it. It's quite frowned upon in the world of surfing—unless of course it's your local wave, you're the better surfer, they pissed you off or did something dumb earlier, you simply don't like them, or any other righteous excuse you can come up with. They're *your* waves after all, *not* theirs.

of the vastly intimidating "Who do you know here??" and "You think you drink a lot??" comments at 19-year-old university parties. Maybe even more similar to four-year-olds at daycare: "Hey I'm playing with all these toys! They're mine! Go find your own!"

October 17, 2019

One of my best friends flew out to hang with me for the weekend. He asked me to be his best man at his wedding! Super amped. It should be an entertaining contrast in front of the wedding guests. The groom: clean-cut, firmly planted in a successful commercial real estate track, with a dog, and a new wife. The guy to his side: sand and saltwater dripping out of his sunburned nose with his home parked in front of the church.

October 19, 2019

Played 18 holes at the Seascape Golf Club with a threesome who were knockin' back drinks earlier. Two of them were closer to my age and the other was probably in his sixties. I was playing well, picking up momentum, until we started on the back nine. The 10th hole is a par 5 that tees off next to the clubhouse through a long, pretty straight valley. The fairway is protected on both sides by relatively steep hills, maybe 60 to 100 feet tall. One of the guys looks at me and slurs, "This is where you send it."

In nearly all circumstances, "sending it," or trying to hit the golf ball as far as you can, is an awful idea, which generally ends with your ball traveling 45 degrees in the wrong direction toward a nearby highway or other group of golfers. Unable to resist the challenge, however, I proceeded to hit the ball as hard as I could and slice it—oh, I don't know—maybe six miles to the right. Hiding my face under my hat, with any possible momentum that I had going for me now gone, the remaining eight holes were a brutal slog. I went from losing zero balls on the front nine to losing a ball every other hole from then on.

On hole 16 or 17, after substantially slowing down our group with my all-star performance, the older guy in the group, sporting a puffy jacket and Gandalf's beard, who had been playing well, nuked a chip over the green into the bushes. Looking directly at me he said, "Man, I *really* hate losing a ball." *Yeah, graybeard? One ball?* My putter all of a sudden felt a lot more like a javelin than a golf club.

October 21, 2019

I made an acquaintance earlier this year with an older gentleman at a wedding shower hosted by my parents. He lives in Santa Cruz, and we bonded over the van I was furnishing at the time and some of my surfboards—namely an experimental wooden Alaia[32] I constructed and a secondhand 9'6" Doug Haut, which was clearly built to charge[33] out-of-my-league Ocean Beach in San Francisco. He was a Kelly's Cove grom[34] back when wetsuits were just coming out and had some fun stories.

He invited me to come surf with him and three other original members of a local surfing club near Pleasure Point. I've always

---

[32] Before the foam surfboards we associate with surfing today, Polynesians had been shaping wooden boards for hundreds, if not nearly thousands, of years. Along with the "Paipo," which is generally around six feet or under and ridden on your belly, the "Alaia" is a longer board, over six feet, which can be ridden on your belly or on your feet. Since there are no fins for stability or maneuvering, the board needs to be thin and narrow, using the rail of the surfboard (the side of it) to slice through and hold in the wave. Gliding down the face of a wave on a 1/2 inch piece of wood you shaped yourself is a pretty great feeling until, of course, the board becomes a wooden missile and comes back at you!

[33] Paddling out to surf big, heavy waves.

[34] A young surfer (though not necessarily a beginner—most of the groms surf better than I ever will).

been told I'm an old soul (though, this is usually contradicted by those same people proceeding to call me a 12-year-old). So I guess I wasn't surprised at how much I enjoyed being out in the water with four guys that averaged probably 75 years of age. Each one riffing quotes from *The Endless Summer*[35] while baiting the others into decades-old inside jokes. "Ah mate, why'd we come out today? You shoulda been here yesterday!" or "Hey look, Jerry's got four fins on his board! So if any of us breaks ours in the water, he has extra! What a good friend." I look forward to paddling out with longtime friends when I'm that age.

---

[35] A 1966 cult classic surf film directed by Bruce Brown.

INTEGRITY

Character is always known. Thefts never enrich; alms never impoverish; murder will speak out of stone walls. The least admixture of a lie—for example, the taint of vanity, any attempt to make a good impression, a favorable appearance—will instantly vitiate the effect. But speak the truth, and all nature and all spirits help you with unexpected furtherance.

— Ralph Waldo Emerson,
Divinity School Address

If I can tell you a small, harmless lie, then I am capable of telling you a large, harmful one. Better to preclude the opportunity. So when I look you in the eyes and speak, know what I say to be true—to the extent that I understand. For if all I have is a corrupt foundation, then all I have will crumble.

You are always aware when you begin to lie. After the first falsification of truth, regardless of whether you deceive yourself about your weight, skill set, or anything else, such a deception may become ingrained in your mind. This is why lying is both so easily prevented and so dangerous at the same time. The first dishonesty is intentional and easy to spot. Over time, however, your distorted truth will become reality. Soon, it may be hard to differentiate between real and fake. At this point, it is not too late to course correct, but it is far harder to bring forth the truth once you have already deceived yourself. Telling the truth from the start is your easiest and best chance for avoiding a downward spiral of lies.

"White lies" are a hypocrisy of intention. You compel yourself to believe that a small deception will not harm anyone. But there is no known calculation for how many little lies it takes to generate a large one, so why provide any ammunition at all? Just one could lead to a cascade. For someone might believe your false truth and carry it toward greater crowds. Worse yet: How are you to know that these small, thought-to-be trivial lies—these small cracks in your foundation that you have *chosen* to chisel out—will not soon follow you inside? When the line blurs, will you falsify the truth in your own home? Will you choose to distort your image to the only person who matters? Will you lie to yourself?

Personal lies are the metastatic tendrils of a disease that you gave yourself. There are no environmental nor genetic factors which predispose a man to such an illness—only personal decisions. Once you witness that you are uttering untruths to yourself, you must realize the severity of the situation. Know that if you are willing, whether out of ignorance or choice, to lie to your own mind, then baseness is quickly approaching and enveloping your very character. For "the corruption of man is followed by the corruption of language."[36] If you are willing to deceive yourself, then you are willing to lie in any other aspect of life as well. Once this disease has taken hold, it is very difficult to cure. You must follow every elusive tentacle of deceit through your mind, searching even for their derivations and evolutions. Then meticulously

---

[36] Ralph Waldo Emerson, *Nature* (Boston & Cambridge: James Munroe and Company, 1849), Chapter IV: Language, para. 7.

remove each deceptive tendril, coiled around the real truths of your conscience.

For years before I was able to admit and harness the truth, I misconstrued to many, including myself, the reason I stopped playing soccer in university. I didn't make the cut as a collegiate athlete, simple as that. I was a smart player, but not quite good enough. This was a painful realization, and it was this pain that caused me to exaggerate the story. Yet it was *far* more agonizing to recognize that I was not willing to come to terms with reality.

However unpleasant, this diagnosis should cause excitement. Unlike the merciless cancers of the body, you can fight the cancers of the mind to any degree that you are willing! The more you fight it, the better you will feel. This effort will bring clarity; the truth that "nothing is at last sacred but the integrity of your own mind."[37] Every action alters the path toward the future you. Honesty lifts you up; dishonesty drags you down. Do not be fooled into thinking otherwise, into thinking that your actions, no matter how small, won't impact your character and your future. The man who exposes his inner lies and decides to fix them knows that he will never revert. There is no chance of going back; the peace of mind found here in this space of honesty is far too rewarding.

One prevailing reason for small lies is lack of knowledge. When we realize that we do not have an answer, we are faced with a decision. Do we accept this truth and move on? Or do we attempt to deceive those around us into believing that we know what we're talking about? Choose wisely. Keeping silent in a manner that mimics understanding, nodding in agreement, ambiguously alluding to what others want to hear even if you know it's

---

[37] Ralph Waldo Emerson, "Self Reliance," in *Essays: First Series* (Boston: J. Munroe and Company, 1847), 44.

not the truth—these are *all* lies. It is understandably uncomfortable to not know something. Unfortunately, our desire to be seen as knowledgeable makes us create omniscient façades. The fact of the matter is that there is far too much information in this world for anyone to know it all. So if someone around you presents themselves with an all-knowing air, you can see through this falsity. It is, after all, a counterproductive behavior. A person of this nature is difficult to be around without questioning the validity of nearly everything that they say.

Instead, think of how natural and easy it is to trust a man who reveals a lack of understanding by asking questions. It is effortless with today's technology to tell someone that you know an answer when you don't. You can act like you're texting, and Google the answer. I know; I've done it many times. And I was always worse off afterward for two reasons. First, I was now expending energy by feeling bad for lying and covering up a lack of knowledge, when I could have been engaging creatively in the conversation. Second, the narrative moves on without me actually understanding the content, and I fall deeper into a hole of dishonesty. This is only one example in the physical world, standing face-to-face with another person. It doesn't even begin to broach our remote interactions online.

Confessing a lack of knowledge is also the most efficient way to obtain it. If your discussion is filled with people saying "Oh yeah, I know what you're talking about" or "Yes, of course," or other similar iterations, it is very likely that the time spent talking is wasted. Neither party gains anything positive at its closure. Instead, a conspicuous feeling will haunt each man's mind that the other is not as he appears. Whereas, a conversation inundated with honest curiosity benefits both participants. They will have gained experience and knowledge, whether through learning new facts or asking further questions. For what is a great meeting of minds if each does not feel their curiosity stronger than before?

The ability to admit not knowing things—*that* is a wonderful expression of integrity. That is the action of an honest person with an aim for real answers and strong relationships. Thus the man who believes that a superficial show of intelligence will take him to great heights has been duped. His peers will find they do not trust him, and his spirit will be wary of his own reflection.

The masses do not thank good, honest men for their actions; they thank these men for their character. "You would compliment a coxcomb doing a good act, but you would not praise an angel."[38] When you are known for your integrity, your honesty will not be seen as an action, but instead as an extension of your prudent character. You will not be seen as the man who did but as the man who *was*.

Understandably, obstacles come with this most involved form of honesty. Mistruth is generally acceptable in society, and you may come across as less polite with your truth. Likewise, admitting disagreement—instead of agreeing to avoid upsetting someone—can bring unpleasantness. Yet, "the truth is handsomer than the affectation of love;" it is better for "your goodness [to] have some edge to it,—else it is none."[39] With the loss of these elements of politeness, you gain solid trust and efficiency. If you know me to be honest in all my words, you will trust what I say to be what I believe, regardless of the outcome or the potential for disagreement.

---

[38] Ralph Waldo Emerson, *An Address Delivered Before the Senior Class in Divinity College*, Cambridge (Boston: James Munroe and Company, 1838), para. 34.
[39] Ralph Waldo Emerson, "Self-Reliance," in *Essays: First Series*. (Boston: J. Munroe and Company, 1847), 45.

Socrates chose his truth instead of his life when given the opportunity to escape his approaching execution. Viktor Frankl chose to stay and endure the brutality of the concentration camp where he was a prisoner, in order to care for and protect his patients. Why? What compels men to take such bold action, which puts them in harm's way, knowing that there is a possible escape?

For both of these men, there was a voice in their minds, which told them what they had to do. We call this voice many names: oracle, divine spirit, our "gut," or maybe inner consciousness. On the road to becoming a Navy SEAL, David Goggins found this voice. He woke up at 24 years old, 300+ pounds, in a dead-end career, facing a life devoid of meaning. He wanted to join the SEALS, but realized he was too weak, mentally and physically. He knew he had to change himself. During this period he faced pain, soreness, and exhaustion. When he found himself wanting comfort instead of his next run in the freezing rain or workout late at night, he became aware of "this voice, [which he had] heard [his] whole life, saying … '*What are you doing? No way man, we gotta go over here.*'"[40] That voice was telling him what he already knew to be true. That if he wanted to toughen up, he had to put himself through a lot of discomfort. He had to brave the uncomfortable as he had never done before. That voice is the one that tells us the real, hard truths. The ones we know, but push back against because they aren't enjoyable to hear.

But is it only those notorious figures such as Socrates, Viktor Frankl, and David Goggins, who braved death or turned around a near-hopeless childhood, who have such a voice? Of course not. As you read this, you know that to be wrong, for it speaks to you,

---

[40] Joe Rogan interview with David Goggins, podcast audio, *The Joe Rogan Experience* #1212 - David Goggins ~00:14:00, December 5, 2018, https://youtu.be/BvWB7B8tXK8

too. This voice inside tells you who you are. What you agree with and what you disagree with. It tells you what actions you have made recently that you disapprove of. It reminds you of events that embarrass you. Not awkward stumbles that produced a laugh, but bigger actions, such as lying or hurting someone. Those events that tear at your heart when you remember them, the pain of which forces your mind elsewhere for a brief moment. You know if you were to have acted rightly in that moment, if you were to have listened to that voice, you would have been better for it. But you did not; so it reminds you that you can do better.

No person can act without fault in every moment; we're human, and we make mistakes. And though this voice may be powerful, it is quiet and easy to avoid if you're not paying attention. With each choice to listen, however, you turn up the volume. You start to realize it is honest and let it take up more space in your mind, even if uncomfortable. And once you have turned the volume up on this inner conscience, once you have amplified it with a megaphone, it can never be turned down. Afterward, you may try to ignore it. But once you realize it's there, that it's wise, that it represents who you *want* to be, you can *never* turn it off.

We erroneously associate heaven and hell with religious or mythical places in space and time. By doing so, we relieve ourselves through the postponement of judgement or by the belief that they are mere illusions—fiction created by the religious. Both of these views are misguided. Heaven and hell are not physical locations, nor are they fables. They are states of *being*. When you pursue deceit, when you seek to undermine, when you intend to harm, hell is not in your future. *Hell is your present.* It is where you exist at this moment. In this state of being, your life attracts guilt, anxiety, depression, and sickness. Such are the poorest of men, wealthy as they may be otherwise.

This is not an eternal sentence, of course. But what does eternity matter when the only experience you have—that of the present—is spent on the low end of the moral spectrum of life? Aim instead toward the potential lightness of this great world through integrity. Ask forthright questions so that you may learn, grow, and uncover the secrets that Mother Nature veils. Speak honestly to garner genuine love with your family and friends. Listen to your own spirit for the peace of a calm mind. Redirect your life toward the heavens.

MY JOURNEY IN PICTURES

Day before setting off

Rainbow Mountain, covered with clouds on the left, and Rainbow Lake in
the middle. Whistler, BC, Canada

Rainbow Lake, Whistler, BC, Canada

Biking around Stanley Park in Vancouver, BC, Canada

Cape Flattery, Washington

Olympic Peninsula, Washington

Puget Sound from Discovery Park, Washington

Indian Beach, Oregon

The very, very secret surf spot at Short Sands Beach in Oregon

Adventure mode in the Siuslaw National Forest

Cape Lookout, Oregon: Disappointingly flat,
after a hike down the hill to the right

Boondocking at the Blue Heron French Cheese Company
in Oregon (check them out!)

On Mt. Scott above Crater Lake, Oregon

The dinner menu for the great white sharks near Bastendorf Beach, Oregon

View of Mount Shasta from Castle Crags, California

A couple months before the trip started, on Green Butte
Ridge, Shasta, California

Camel Rock, Humboldt, California

Big River rivermouth in Mendocino, Northern California

My two sheilas

Next to Jack O'Neill's former house, Pleasure Point,
Santa Cruz, California

The only picture I have of myself surfing during my
10-month surf trip (how fitting)

My good pal showing me how to cast metal rings in Santa Cruz,
California (left); My wetsuit after three years, 273 stitches,
and a bottle of neoprene glue (right)

How could I ever? Santa Cruz, California

Sequoia National Park, California (left);
My wax seal for finishing letters to friends (right)

Alta Peak, Sequoia National Park, California

Drinking hot water to keep warm during a below freezing night in Kings
Canyon, California

Kings Canyon, California

A fun day filled with offshore wind and punchy closeouts
at the Pismo Pier in Central California

Ventura, California

Today 10:42

There's a chance I get to
"work from home" this
afternoon

In which case the reefs
should be fun

Never trust a surfer

North of Kona, the Big Island of Hawaii

First surf on the Seven Mile Miracle—hard to imagine this place exists.
North Shore, Oahu, Hawaii

Morning surf on the North Shore of Oahu, Hawaii

Getting lost in Moanalua Valley, Oahu, Hawaii

Oahu, Hawaii

Find me a good looking tree, and I'll climb it.
Manoa Valley, Oahu, Hawaii

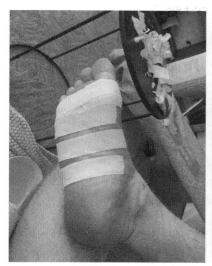

Post-reef dance (left); "Why'd the chicken cross the road?" "'Cause he was goin' home—he local, brah" (right)

Perfect Ehukai sandbars on the North Shore of Oahu (left); My wonderful, beautiful mom in Honolulu for the (disappointing) Super Bowl LIV! (right)

First day cruising around Australia

The Surf Flex Lab, Wollongong, NSW, Australia (left);
Snapped my stick bodysurfing in Newcastle, NSW, Australia (right)

One pretty Uruguayan girl and one fantastic beach,
somewhere near Byron Bay, NSW, Australia

A handsome bluebottle with a 45+ foot long stinger, Byron Bay,
NSW, Australia

"I'll take a double espresso, and my board will have a cappuccino" (left);
One big night (right). Both in Brisbane.

My travel companions on the train (left) to Noosa Heads,
QLD, Australia (right)

The act of finding a beautiful hidden point break might be as exhilarating as surfing it. Location: wouldn't you like to know?

Last day in Noosa Heads before trekking back to Sydney for my flight to the states

Posing to take pictures of myself for no real reason makes me
uncomfortable … so here's to making myself uncomfortable.
Noosa Heads, QLD, Australia

ALONE AT THE SUMMIT

Central California and the Sierra

October 27th, 2019

Even though it's large, California is a crowded state. And since people flock to live near water, there aren't too many spots left with good surf where you can feel like you're removed from civilization. Even if you get decently far out of the way, you're almost always within earshot of cars buzzing down the freeway or people walking on the beach.

One region with plenty of opportunity to be alone is Big Sur. And there's something about that remoteness that amplifies your awareness. Increased speeds and elevated heights make you feel more alive. A licking from an overhead wave in chilly, grey water seems a bit more violent, a trace colder, a shade darker.

October 28th, 2019

While driving through the central valley, completely by accident, I ended up passing through Lemoore, California. Cruising by the city limit sign, I thought to myself, "Lemoore ... Lemoore ... what is in Lemoore ... Oh. Wait. Kelly's wave pool?" American professional surfer Kelly Slater constructed the "perfect" wave, a beautiful combination of engineering and surfing, at his Surf Ranch out in the middle of the central valley. Mapping the location, I saw that I was only two miles away. Naturally, I drove over to see if I could check it out. Unlikely, since it costs thousands to get in, but I had to at least try. Standing in front of the closed, wooden gate, my conversation with the security guard went something like:

"Hi!"
"What do you want?"
"Well ... I know I can't surf it ... but can I see it?"
"No."
"Please?"
"No."
"How about for $20?"
"No."

Okay, I didn't actually try to bribe him, but I should have.

October 29th, 2019

October in Santa Cruz is a dream. The mix of remaining summer south swells with the start of the winter north swells means non-stop decent-to-good surf. And if you're on a surf trip and there's surf ... you surf. A month without much rest had me exhausted, and my paddling technique and posture went out the door. And because of the month-long abuse, my left shoulder started bothering me. So I decided to give my body a break and cruise to the Sierra for some late season hiking.

It seems my trips to the mountains always draw out some form of connection to my grandfather on my dad's side. Even though we never met, our (apparently) similar attitudes and appreciation for nature formed a bond between us. He spent a great deal of time in this area and, as a young man, planted a sequoia tree in a distinct spot, which my father once showed me. Nearly one hundred feet tall now, the tree is by no means hidden, yet its history will remain a mystery for most who pass by it. It only seems fitting that for the next several nights, I'll be sleeping next to this sequoia. Planting a tree—what a simple and wonderful way to leave a legacy in a place you love.

October 31st, 2019

Late fall in the mountains couldn't be any more perfect. The foliage is breathtaking as patches of the forest turn from dark green to warm yellows and oranges. Barring the smoke from an occasional fire, the air is crisp, maybe a bit thin, but refreshing and perfect for hiking. Lastly, and most importantly, it's extremely cold. Though no snow yet, the nights are well below freezing, and the days are barely warm enough for you to thaw out. Being cold all day makes people uncomfortable, and there's a direct relationship between how comfortable an area is and the amount of people who venture toward it. All the better.

I hiked up to Alta Peak today completely alone. Fourteen miles of uninterrupted bliss. At the outset, I was greeted by several ushers of the forest. A family of mule deer welcomed me to the great concert hall that was to be my home for the remainder of the day. As my body warmed up from movement, my feet strummed a slow adagio through the woods. The first sequence of switchbacks a scale to which Nature set its tune. And with each change in elevation, a new set of musicians. The rush of forest rivers changing to the trickle of mountain streams; the wind passing through dense woods to the swaying of uncrowded trees; the whistle of stellar jays and the beat of woodpeckers to the cries of soaring birds of prey. The great granite conductors above led the ensemble, which held its harmony for hours as I marched.

Gaining elevation, the melody weakened as the forest attenuated until all was quiet above the treeline. Only several short, thickset sequoias were dispersed among the quartz and beige-grey granite ter-rain of the mountain, their trunks a dozen feet in diameter. This sud-den diminuendo left only the wind as a background to my steps, like the suspenseful vibrations of air that follow the striking of a cymbal.

Atop the summit, as my footsteps halted their progression, even the tremor of the wind relaxed. An intermission below the purest blue sky one could imagine. Not a single cloud above the entirety of the visible mountain range. Across the Sierra, Mount Whitney sang the crescendo of her own siren song. Though I have heard it before, at this moment I was too far away from its tempta-tions. Occasionally a bird's call from the orchestra below made its way up to me, enticing me to leave the silence for the melody of the forest below. But I sat for a while—for who ever wants to leave a mountain summit?

Fueled by a handful of cashews and some fresh water, I eventu-ally called out goodbyes to my mountain friends. Though sluggish from the rest and warm afternoon sun, my feet began a quicker tempo this time, plucking a sprightly andante as I reentered the forest. The players rested in the shade from their morning perfor-mance. I hiked home in a quiet trance, across the mountainside, over the ridgeline, and through the forest.

Just before exiting the trail, the first person I'd seen that day stumbled around the corner. On his way to set camp for the night, I said hello. I hope that he will appreciate tomorrow's symphony as much as I did today's.

November 11th, 2019

I've discovered that, for me, one of the most attractive things a woman can say is, "I'm turning off my phone; I've got work to do." I love when independent people know their time is valuable and spend it well.

November 16th, 2019

My first surf session after two weeks of rest coincided with a week-end of overhead waves and offshore wind in Jalama, near Point Conception. I mapped it and drove out there, planning to spend the next couple of days surfing and relaxing on the beach. Jalama is relatively equidistant from San Luis Obispo and Santa Barbara, and decently far off of Highway 101. Barring the massive and packed campground, with just one general store for miles around and no cell-service, it has a pretty remote feeling to it. That's difficult to find on the California coast.

The reef break at the south end of Jalama Beach, named Tarantulas, was packed with incredible surfers. So I chose a sandbar peak closer to the parking lot, in front of the campground. It was less consistent, and the shape wasn't nearly as good, but it was still hollow and only a couple guys were in the water. During my first try paddling out, I learned that it was substantially more powerful than I thought, and I got drilled and swiftly washed back to shore. On my second try, I successfully caught a rip current and was out back,[41] behind the waves, pretty quickly. Sitting in the water for the first time in weeks, the surf seemed a bit daunting. But after one good wave and one good wipeout, I felt comfortable again. And after a couple more rides, I was pretty much euphoric.

Then, at the bottom of the fourth wave that morning, the corner of it closed out on me, and I bailed off my board to try and dive underneath. Coming off several bumps at the bottom of the wave, I was a bit off balance and ended up falling forward instead

---

[41] Getting "out back" means paddling out behind where the waves are breaking. Generally speaking, a surfer will sit just behind where the waves are breaking (outside of them), until the right one comes. Since water in rip currents flows back out to sea, you can sometimes use them to get out behind the surf.

of dropping straight down. After three or four seconds tumbling around underwater, a sharp object torpedoed—or at least that's how it felt—through my lower lip, into my bottom teeth. By falling forward, my board ended up pointing directly at me and the tension in my leash slingshotted it back, straight toward my face. Still seconds from coming up for air, I panicked a bit but stayed calm enough to get to the surface before the next wave of the set. I pulled at my board, stuck in some kelp, which became dislodged only after the next wave pounded down on my head. After that, finally freed, I was violently washed back to the beach.

I was in a state of shock and expected my face to be covered in blood as I gasped for air, crawling up the beach, people running over and staring at me. But the obvious consequence of being alone is that no one is watching out for you. Likewise, all of the struggle had happened underwater and, though it still felt like it, the nose of my board had not actually pierced my lip. With no blood and my breath calm again, I saw the 20 or so people in sight simply going about their day, oblivious to my struggles.

In minutes, my hair still sopping wet, without consciously deciding anything, I was in my van driving back over the hill away from the beach. I ran away from the scene as fast as possible. Nothing bad had really happened. Only a slight bruise on my lower lip, which you would only notice if you were looking for it. And maybe I'm a bit weak for my reaction. Regardless, my mind went wild. First, I was overcome with relief—physically, I was completely fine. Then came fear. I realized that a couple inches in another direction, and I could have lost an eye. If the board hadn't hit my lip first or if my mouth had been open, I could have seriously damaged my teeth. Lower toward my throat and, simply put, it could have stopped my breathing. Then came anxiety over all those possibilities. Then relief again that they didn't happen. Anger for putting myself in the situation. Denial that it had actually happened. Joy that I made the right decision to leave immediately turned to guilt for running away from good surf and my plans for the weekend. Grateful that everything was alright and then disgusted at myself for trivializing the possible harm I avoided. In minutes, this train of emotions shot through my head like fucking lightning bolts.

I called one of my best friends to get my mind off it. Then my mom. And then, two hours later, as addicts do to soothe their pain from an addiction, I paddled out to surf down south at Campus Point near UCSB. The waves there were small and mellow. And I stayed in the water all afternoon. Aaaallll afternoon. Until the sun went down. And until, even in my 3/2mm wetsuit in the warmer Santa Barbara water, I was cold ... and content ... and numb.

GRATEFULNESS

People don't appreciate the lack of mosquitos
as much as they should.[42]

— Mark Mitchell

The word privilege has deteriorated in the modern world. A line has been drawn that divides niches of humanity from all others. The implication is that those who do not benefit from certain advantages have no privileges. And yet ... you breathe, do you not? And so I ask, how many ever truly appreciate the experience that it is to live?

Each morning the masses wake up and immediately go about their routines. Where is that moment of wonder, which, even if only ephemeral, should happen each and every day? Where we all realize the magnificence of the basic phenomena of life. Where we admire the sunrise or revere the stars. Where we shiver from the birds' song. Find me a man who wakes up with conscious love for the beating of his physical heart, and I will show you what good fortune looks like.

---

[42] My father, as we hiked with a view of the Minarets in the Sierra while being swarmed by mosquitos.

You do not have the right to be loved, to be paid for work, or to be treated justly. You do not have the right to act individually. To my fellow countrymen: You do not have the right to speak against your government, to protest, nor to carry a weapon. You do not even have the right to breathe. For you have no rights—you have only privileges. That any of these privileges be written into law is an astounding accomplishment of society, but do not let it fool you into the belief that life itself has entitled them to you. Do not take for granted these wonders. Do not take for granted your ability to act independently, to decide how to see the world, and to choose how to live.

We can all recede into our own minds and remember something that we adore. We may all be grateful for that which life has bestowed upon us forevermore. We should all listen to John Muir's words, which make me light and joyful at my core:

> *The trees round about them seem as perfect in beauty and form as the lilies, their boughs whorled like lily leaves in exact order. This evening, as usual, the glow of our camp-fire is working enchantment on everything within reach of its rays. Lying beneath the firs, it is glorious to see them dipping their spires in the starry sky, the sky like one vast lily meadow in bloom!* ***How can I close my eyes on so precious a night?***[43]

I hike in the Sierra for more than a view of mountains and forests. I travel through them with feelings of gratitude for the privilege it is to view such grandeur. I am not in awe of the faces of the granite walls of Yosemite. I am in awe of the fortune I have

---

[43] John Muir, *My First Summer in the Sierra* (Boston and New York: Houghton Mifflin Company, 1917), Chapter 4, "July 9," para. 6. My formatting.

to see those exhilarating palisades. The euphoria! Sit me under a strong sugar pine with only sturdy feet to keep me grounded and light to illuminate my path, and I will be satisfied.

It is in nature that we should encounter landscapes that make us rethink the priority and worth of our material possessions. For in my life, I have never known a place more sacred than a redwood forest. I would rather chance the odds of staring Medusa in the eyes than looking up in an old *Sequoia sempervirens* grove. Frozen by awe, I might stand for eternity. My only true fault in walking through such a forest is that I cannot gaze up upon each tree for forever. By the grace of God I may feel! If that is all in this life, then so be it, because that is enough.

Breathe! Breathe in the beautiful world through your eyes and the resounding world through your ears. Deeply fill your lungs and release each inhalation with the hope that life will grant you the privilege to do it again. The breath inward is a vessel for life.

Likewise, the breath outward is a vessel for gratitude. Upon release, each inhalation may be turned into love, thanks, friendship, or apology. One common form of spoken appreciation takes the shape of prayer. I find prayers to be a disputed matter. Granted, my understanding of religious faiths is novice; I have no expertise on the subject. To my amateur eye, though, praying to make a request does nothing but bear one's weight upon another, be that a god or a man. The only time I understand the words of a prayer to be any more pious than other speech is when I feel thankfulness behind them.

These are prayers driven by an appreciation for the current state of being. Witnessing the rising sun polish and glaze a dark orange chaparral-laden landscape in red-rock Sedona, I found myself whispering under my breath, "Thank you for waking me up and allowing me to see another beautiful day." Was this acknowledgement directed at God, the sun, or myself, I do not know, but I am *certain* that it was composed in prayer.

From the intense volcanic reds of the Amarillo to the sublime pinks and greens of the North Shore. The reflection of the sun's light off of the desert floor or glossy silent water. Laughs from the families near me. Light winds heard off in the brush or above the palms before feeling them on my skin and in my hair. The great, full breath when I have cast off the problems of the day. The shiver down my spine when I lie still in that moment. It is here that I know how to pray. It is here that such words displace more room in the world with their increased weight.

I understand the desire to supplicate during times of great stress and fear. I would never yield that a man cannot feel the need for help from a higher power. And such an action could be a helpful step in finding one's way. But I still think it leads in the wrong direction. Begging for forgiveness, for help, or for strength removes a sense of self from the situation. It may be more tough to take the entire weight of your struggle on your own shoulders. However, we must find our own path through times of difficulty.

On the list of difficult experiences that life brings, encounters with loss easily find themselves near the top. They are affairs that everyone will endure, regardless of their status in life. Maybe through the death of a loved one, the end of a relationship, the completion of an important project, or the disruption of a great living situation. These events may be the most heart-wrenching ordeals you face. And though I could never boast any remedy for their pain, I do believe that there is one preferable approach to handling them.

Be grateful for the ways that this person or these experiences changed you. Think of the things you learned from them or of the experiences of love you shared with them. Love, though sometimes fleeting, is a most extraordinary experience that we are fortunate to feel. When a close friend's long-term relationship ended, I wrote him:

I'm sorry to hear about your breakup. Having been in a similar situation, I know it's hard. It's tough to lose your best friend ... and maybe even more difficult to say that statement out loud. It's hard to be alone after having that close companion for so long. Something that has helped me, which I now believe to be the only good way to deal with such a situation, is appreciation for the wonderful experiences of the relationship. And no, I'm not asking you to dwell on all the memories and send her a text with all the things you miss about her. Instead, when you think of memories involving her, take a moment to appreciate them. Be grateful for the wonderful times you shared. It's a tremendous opportunity to feel something so intimate and special with another person. Maybe it isn't meant to be, and she isn't the one. But you'll always have those memories and experiences that made you a better person and might even inform a future where you find the woman who is right for you. It gets easier to deal with the loss. As long as you don't suppress the negative emotions, they'll relax in time. And you know what, maybe it will be her, but for right now, it sounds like it's not. That's tough to deal with, but stay strong and appreciative and keep working on yourself. There's no better investment than that. I don't think anything else can lead us more directly to fulfilled and happy lives.

Could I ever compare the feeling of losing a girlfriend to the death of a mother or child? Of course not. But it should not be our aim to compare that which two people feel, even under similar experiences. We are all wired differently, and there is no need to contrast the type or amount of pain between you and me. Instead, take your own independent experience and find the wonder in it. I can't imagine any better approach to loss than celebrating the person who has left our lives or this world! Extol the reasons they impacted you and the love you know you will always have for them.

It occurs to me that this same notion can be applied not only to loss, but also to the world's current struggles.

Genius always looks forward.
The eyes of man are set in his forehead, not in his hindhead.
Man hopes. Genius creates.[44]

It is well understood that our physical actions cause some of the planet's problems. I believe that the reason for those actions is a disconnect with nature—the physical and real earth whose sustenance and resources make our lives so easy. The civilized patron eats his steak with fork and knife, napkin squarely on lap, with appreciation for the chef and extreme prejudice toward the hunter. The hunter eats his steak out of respect and thanks for the animal's life that he took.

Who is the real savage here? The man who kills what he needs to survive, who sees the life which he takes, and feels an emotional connection to it? The one who might forever remember that animal's actual face, the contours of its eyes, and the feel of its skin? Or the man who eats that same meat with complete disconnect from the life that was given to nourish his body? The same one whose eyes would

---

[44] Ralph Waldo Emerson, "The American Scholar," *Essays* (New York: Charles E. Merrill & Co., 1907) para. 15. My formatting.

never be caught watching the slaughter in progress, as if the taking of life is beneath him, even when he benefits from it. If everyone had to kill the animals whose meat they eat, there would be far less consumed and a much stronger appreciation for it as nourishment.

This theme has many parallels. For water, for littering, for deforestation, and for so much more. Don't stop your shower short for fear of drought; stop it short out of respect for where the water comes from! Climb the great mountains whose snowfall fills our reservoirs and cisterns. Observe that mountainous meltwater and runoff, which falls on command from our faucets, and you will *feel* why it should not be wasted. "How rich our inheritance in these blessed mountains, the tree pastures into which our eyes are turned!"[45] May we all regularly embody John Muir's gratitude for the wild—that one may recognize the world he lives in to be his most precious fatherly bequest. The entitled American expects clean water as a right and does not understand that it is yet another privilege. The great, green-focused Los Angeles screams "Draught!" as it erects more skyscrapers and broadens its boundaries. A magnificent desert metropolis that sucks the Sierra and Colorado bone dry.

Be thankful. It is such a small request. Realize the incredible gifts that are the earth and nature and simply appreciate that we get to live in such beauty. Find wonder, not monotony, in the simple things that you expect every day—water, food, warmth, daylight, breath. Do not feel entitled to these gifts.

I've seen a common trend of people wanting to eliminate conventional technologies or practices in the name of conservation and the health of our planet. I understand the sentiment, yet I disagree with the method. Closely associated with this movement is usually

---

[45] John Muir, *My First Summer in the Sierra* (Boston and New York: Houghton Mifflin Company, 1917), Chapter 2, "June 15," para. 3.

a polarized environment of outrage. Such are those who shout to destroy everything that is having a negative environmental impact right now. This is where gratefulness plays an important role by slowing the mind. *The future is not backwards.* Calm your anger on the subject and be thankful. For example, many dams have been beneficial by providing us energy and water—not all, as recent investigation has found out, but many. Now with that frame of mind, can we find a better solution for systems that can damage the earth? Can technology advance the nature of dams, for instance, to generate hydroelectric power in a more environmentally-friendly way?

The world may be in a constant flux, just as our views of it are. However, according to Hans Rosling's book *Factfulness*, statistics show that the constant change in many measures, from poverty to education and access to medical care, is trending in a generally positive direction.[46] Industrial society is in its youth in the context of the timeline of humanity, and we are just starting to understand our errors. Yes, we must act quickly. More importantly, we must act insightfully. To run without thought in the wrong direction is to distance yourself further from the solution. With a grateful outlook, we may take the wasted energy of our anger and anxiety and use it to labor *together* on methods that will actually aid and conserve our earth!

I distract, however, from my main focus. Gratefulness is not just a mindset for dealing with loss or for making progress in the world. It is, more importantly, the start of a journey toward fulfillment. One wonderful method for experiencing satisfaction in life is spending time bringing joy to others. Paying forward your own appreciation by offering a compassionate hand to those who

---

[46] Hans Rosling, *Factfulness* (New York: Flatiron Books, 2018). If you feel overwhelmed by a negative outlook on the world, this book will provide you with a well-supported argument to change that view.

may need it. I have heard this stated best in Dr. Thomas Starzl's memoir: "One by one, my patients would save me by letting me help them."[47] I know of no greater method for finding contentment than through efforts that positively impact the people and situations around me. Be selfish by being selfless.

Though I spent only a brief two years volunteering in hospice care, I found more joy in the experience than I ever expected. That happiness, along with the skills I acquired, was greater payment than I could have asked for.

There are environments in life that feel unique because it is difficult to believe they existed before you encountered them and heartbreaking to think you may never experience them again. The compassionate environment I found myself in while training to be a hospice volunteer was exactly that. To the passing eye, the sight would have been mundane: Two dozen strangers sitting and talking in a conference room. For me as a participant, however, it was electric. It was a group of people engrossed in learning about life's most intense transitional period: death.

How to interact with the dying? How to comfort them? How *not* to instruct them, for how could you ever give advice to the dying on how to die? From my experience, the most common form of appreciation when encountering death is the newfound, or rather newly remembered, appreciation for the basic act of living. While this is not at all trivial, I have encountered deeper appreciations beyond enjoying the present. I subjectively define them as deeper for their more personal and detailed existence.

Among these was gratefulness for the personal bond created with any given patient. I had the privilege of hearing accounts

---

[47] Thomas E. Starzl, *The Puzzle People: Memoirs of a Transplant Surgeon* (Pittsburgh: University of Pittsburgh Press, 2003), 198.

ranging from the most mundane to the most affecting. Stories of what they had for dinner, of seashells collected, of job promotions, of unsolved family strife, and of wars fought in misty jungles. Independently, each account was interesting. But as a whole, the act of listening to and feeling these stories amassed the epic of a person's life. It built a foundation for trust that I am still grateful for, even after these patients' passing.

From those connections, I gained far more than I gave. Receiving their trust and creating that bond with each patient, even if only fleeting in the physical world, brought me real joy, which I actively carry into other realms of my life. This is a very specific experience to me, and each pair of individuals in every union will have a different one. Ah! The unlimited possibilities of the human experience are a wonder! Each man, by giving a bit of time and effort to another who needs it, will find himself impacted in an unexpectedly positive manner. Influenced in an individual way that can only be attributed to that *one person*. Create a unique life by helping others. Create a better version of yourself by helping others. *Help yourself by helping others.*

I must briefly digress once again to present an example of this self-help through action. My eye has always been drawn toward the handwritten letter. I relish in the choreography of ink, a delightful dance upon each page that expresses far more than the words themselves. Every letter is an extension of the man who writes it, as if the ink were his blood and the paper his flesh. The texture of it, its weight in your hands, its existence only for specific pairs of eyes, its permanence in space. It all feels grand to me. I could not express why until I read the following, several years back:

> ... *Our tokens of compliment and love are for the most part barbarous. Rings and other jewels are not gifts, but apologies for gifts. The only gift is a portion of thyself. Thou must bleed*

for me. Therefore the poet brings his poem; the shepherd, his lamb; the farmer, corn; the miner, a gem ... This is right and pleasing, for it restores society in so far to its primary basis, when a man's biography is conveyed in his gift ... [48]

I write because it is one of the only ways I know to present a part of myself to another. Each letter is a personal and creative part of me and takes several hours of my time. To start, my works were generally given solely for thanks. To former teachers and mentors and friends for their impact on me. Over the years, these letters—of which I have proudly amassed a great many—have evolved into something more. They are intended to deliver not only my thanks, but my thoughts, my feelings, my experiences, and my interests strictly for the benefit of the reader.

Reflecting upon this effort, it has become apparent that I, most likely, receive more from writing them than the recipients may gain from acquiring them. I believe that this is symbolic for all acts of real giving. Those who give truly tend to receive more than they could have ever expected in return. From these letters I have gained friendship, trust, philosophy, insight, feedback, and love. I have written passages that still impact me, years later, both through their words and my reaction to their words. Imagine that! Pouring your heart out to someone else, for no other reason than to appreciate them, and, in turn, finding yourself the most impacted?

Furthermore, these acts of selfless giving lead us to genuine connection. This is embodied well by the conclusion of a letter written by a friend in response to my own: "I really wanted you to know all this ... [and] I have to say, this sounds more like a love

---

[48] Ralph Waldo Emerson, "Gifts," *Essays: Second Series* (Boston: James Munroe and Company, 1844), 175-176.

letter [than I intended it to be]." When two people give freely, when "the flowing of the giver unto me, [is] correspondent to my flowing unto him. When the waters are at level," we find love.[49] We find love because we have both acted toward each other out of love.

Lastly, this collection of letters I have written serves as an archive for past states of being. Much like a picture album. They bring me back to the grief or pride I felt in that time because I was willing to express those emotions in ink. They take me back to the moments when I pondered what to write, when I made slight edits, or when I decided how much of myself I would entrust to that person.

In the beginning, it was unbeknownst to me that writing these letters would have such a considerable personal impact and strengthen many of my close bonds. It simply seemed a prudent thing to do at the time. This is a beautiful secret of nature. That a value's true worth is found only after it has been acted out and experienced. That is to say: I have only discovered the impact that gratitude has on me—the peace it brings me, the mindset it armors me with, the presence it shares with me—*once I have already lived with it*. Once I have expressed it from a summit in the form of a prayer. Once I have cherished those who I have lost and all they have given me. Once I have teared up at the sight of devastated nature. Once I have held out my hand and written my name in love. So, let Homer's formulae embolden Odysseus as resourceful and Penelope as wise. I would be proud for my epithet to simply read: Grateful.

---

[49] Ralph Waldo Emerson, "Gifts," *Essays: Second Series* (Boston: James Munroe and Company, 1844), 177.

ACCORDING TO PLAN

Southern California

November 26th, 2019

One autumn evening, home for Thanksgiving, I found myself wandering at night through a redwood grove. Opportunities to be in danger in this environment are almost nonexistent, save for a bit of poison oak or tripping over something on the ground. But I still feel it instinctive to be on guard while alone in the dark. Especially when the thick canopy blocks most of the moonlight from the forest floor. Even the occasional small animal scurrying around is enough to make my mind alert.

As I cautiously continued further away from the path and past the grove, the gaps in the trees started to let in a bit more light on the ground. I could hear the slight whimper of some baby animals in the bushes around 40 feet in front of me. Then, next to the bush, a jet black creature, maybe a foot tall in the dark, started to make a substantial amount of noise. I halted in my tracks. It slowly moved in my direction and then proceeded to charge. I caught a glance of the white line down its back, kicked up some rocks and dirt in its direction, and ran away with a yelp. Not today, my friend!

December 2nd, 2019

I jumped into the water south of Scripps Pier before the sun rose this morning. There were definitely a few surfers already in the water, but in the darkness, I couldn't tell how many. As the light filtered into the sky, I realized that there were a hundred or so people, spread out over a couple hundred yards. And I thought Santa Cruz was crowded! Surfing in southern California must be what driving through New York City feels like.

December 7th, 2019

I fight with a dilemma posed by surfing. On one hand, it's good exercise, a fun activity, and a cool way to meet new people. On the other hand, it is a uselessly hedonistic pursuit. Barring maybe if someone's drowning in the ocean—a surfer does have a better chance than most of saving them. So … why do it? Why spend so much time devoted to something that is quite selfish in nature?

Part of it, if not the entirety of it, is this feeling that I can only describe with an example. I can be having an awful month—one where nothing is going my way, and I'm kind of grumpy and tired. And then the surf picks up, and I paddle out and catch one good wave. Not a dozen, not a handful, just one. One solid wave with enough energy to push into some big turns where you feel the power of the ocean transferred to your body.

The moment I come over the shoulder of that ride, I'm no longer having a bad month. I'm walking back to my car saying "Hi!" to everyone I pass, I'm singing to myself, I'm looking like an idiot trying to whistle even though I know I can't. I go back to the exact same work I was procrastinating beforehand with a joyful and more efficient perspective. My shoulders are tight and sore from the workout, yet at the same time are completely and entirely relaxed. My breathing is deeper and my ability to listen to others is sharper. Simply put, sometimes I don't stop smiling for several days because of one good wave. Whatever *that* is—that's why I do it.

December 15th, 2019

Easily the most dangerous stretch of road I've covered over the last two or three thousand miles of driving, which includes some solid stretches on forest service roads, has to be Highway 101 from Carlsbad to Cardiff. One more group of girls changing into their "wetsuits" on the side of the highway, and I may accidentally drive into the ocean.

December 18th, 2019

I lucked into a spot in Solana Beach for the past two weeks and was fortunate enough to have a view of a couple surf breaks in the area. Several good-sized swells rolled through while I was here, and it's been fun analyzing the different waves that break over a single reef, depending on the conditions. The swell's direction, period, and size, the wind, the tide, the size and shape of the reef—it all affects how a spot works. A two-foot change in tide could mean the difference between a mushy, slow rolling entry into a wave and a steep drop into a shallow-water guillotine.

One part of a surf break that seems valuable to analyze before paddling out is the white water. For a reef break, one long line of white bubbles angled 45 degrees toward the shore means that the wave will continue to break down the line without interruption. The angle of the white water correlates to the velocity the surfer needs to cruise down the unbroken part of the wave. The closer the angle gets to 0 degrees, the more speed you need. When it reaches 0 degrees, or rather when the white water is parallel to the beach, there is a boundary between "sections"—each section being an area on the wave to maneuver. This might be a place that you need to speed by before it closes off the next section, preventing you from continuing down the wave. Or, it could be one where the water starts to heave over itself, creating a cavity for the rider to pull into—the infamous "barrel." A hollow pocket of air surrounded by water moving toward the sky on one side of you before falling toward the ocean again on the other. Created by Mother Nature for absolutely no other reason than for wave riders to glide through. The aim is to slide into this little tube of air and then come out before it closes.

This particular break in Solana Beach can be ridden right or left. At shoulder high to a foot overhead, around low tide, the right was a bit steep at the beginning, then slowed and turned into a long, open face to cruise up and down. On the left, the paddle in was more drawn out, giving maybe even an extra second to get into the wave and pop up. For another 25 yards—about two to three seconds—it rolls casually. At that point, the next 10 yards of water jack up at the same time, creating a moving wall in the direction you're traveling. Sometimes it crumbles in a way that you have to straighten out to shore. Other times the wall pitches over itself with enough room to step on the gas and ride through. Depending on the skill of the surfer, this can end two different ways: 1) by getting barrelled, riding through the pocket of air created by the wave as previously mentioned, or 2) by getting detonated, demolished by the wave falling on your head. I usually elect for the first option and end up with the second, not having a choice in the matter.

For one particular swell, I had the luck to watch it rise over the course of a couple hours. An offshore storm close to the coast of California built up rapidly. The waves created by the storm arrived on shore before the storm itself. I have never lived close enough to the ocean to actually appreciate the quickness with which surf can build. In a matter of hours, the surf went from almost completely flat to well overhead.

It's wild to watch this energy come from what seems like nowhere. No change in weather or anything that might tip someone off who didn't check the forecast or see the news. Just the occasional frontrunner, one set of waves much larger than the current ones, which arrives at the shore hours before the swell is supposed to. These are like Mother Nature's warning that something menacing is on its way. The experience makes me want to set up shop next to a specific surf break in the future. To observe and learn all its quirks and tricks.

December 28th, 2019

Before I went to the airport yesterday, my mom made a jokingly eloquent comment, "For not having a plan, it seems like everything is going according to one!" It's the first time in my life that I've prioritized the current moment over future ones. And, somehow, it seems like it's working out. The feeling of getting on the plane to Hawaii was the same one I felt when I got into my van the first time. Like I'm getting away with something.

I've changed the answer to my friends' questions on my intended destination. I went north. Then I went south. Now I'm going west. Y'all are welcome.

RESILIENCE

Warm to cold, a crimson blue,
Wind delivered by another hue;
Fast to slow, a risen mind,
Thoughts I received from the greater bind;
Past to peer, and neither's right,
Here I exist in the brightest night.[50]

— "Afterglow"

Imagine that when you die, you arrive at heaven's gates. In front of the divine entryway stands a person who looks familiar. Hesitantly, you proceed closer. And when you reach this person, you feel the odd sensation that you are standing in front of a curious mirror. That this person is *you*—but not exactly. They appear to stand a bit taller. Their character exudes confidence and calmness; their eyes seem to gleam from the pride of a life well-lived. And in this moment, they speak, "Hello, I am the representation of who God intended you to become."

As you converse, you see the circumstances that led you away from this person who stands before you. The chances you let pass

---

[50] I wrote this poem in the margins of Emerson's essay "Experience" as the brisk summer winds of the Bay Area relaxed into the night.

by and the times where you let others manipulate you. The occasions where you knew you should have acted differently, and the person you could've been had you acted more prudently. Laying on your deathbed, you felt that you had tried your best, yet now you question that conclusion.

Is this the only way that such a meeting could come to pass? What actions could you take, what opportunities could you seize, and what limits could you eclipse that would change the course of this encounter? Imagine, instead, walking up to this champion, whose life God himself conceived, and when you meet face-to-face, you see a slight note of wonder in their eyes. They're alarmed because you, who walk before them, appear to carry yourself even more proudly than they. Startled during conversation because your accomplishments reached beyond their own dreams. Ecstatic that they had more to offer. Honored to see that potential in the flesh. Curious where on earth you found the inspiration to pursue such character.[51]

There are a series of places I have encountered in the world where I feel the combination of an air of tranquility and gravity. During difficult times or while pondering important decisions, I have found myself in these spots almost without remembering that I chose to be there. Redwood groves, secret beaches, mountain summits, imposing courtyards, and benches with a lofty view of the west, to name a few. Their beauty and grandeur emanate an ambience of importance.

After minutes of quiet in these environments, however, I realize that it is not their physical attributes which overpower me. It is the sensation of their impermanence. Even the most monumental of mountains will erode, toppled by the trials of time. No matter how grand these settings may be, they will all change and

---

[51] Adapted from a story told by David Goggins

expire—as will I. This is a sensation I can only describe as "feeling mortal." And through these moments where I feel the temporality of life, I experience great excitement. For the understanding that I only have a limited amount of time left on earth is, in parallel, the understanding that I still have time to spend.

To know that you will die is to acknowledge the privilege that you have the opportunity to live. The only mistake made here is not living with that mentality every day. Not as a matter of focus, but as a matter of direction.

Let this not be a catalyst of fear, though; let it be one of excitement! Act now with your values in the forefront of every intention so that you may rejoice in your final moments. You may not reach the ideal because that very well may not be possible. But, at the end of your days, your inner voice will shout out, "*That* is how a life is lived! I have loved, fought, connected, and thought, all in undoubted sincerity. I have left everything on the table. I gave the world my finest gift: All of me."

Live this idea every day, too! When each night falls and your eyes rest, let your last thoughts be those of reflective joy. "*That* is how a day is done! It could not have been done better! Maybe not in result, but in intention, I was perfect." To live with your mortality as a guidepost means not only striving for larger impact, but also closing each day knowing it was well spent and that you acted truly and spoke honestly.

To prevail on this front, you must take risks. I request that the world advocates for all people to take risks that will make them feel alive. I request that parents not only let their kids explore, but also lead them to explore. I request that we actively seek out for ourselves the opportunities this world has to offer. Let adventurers slide off the sides of grand mountains, paddle through shark infested waters, freeze at the Poles, and disappear into dark forests. If you believe that your fear for another's safety should supersede their desire to explore, keep it to yourself. *Let them take risks.* Do not be dismayed at these illustrations of great physical danger. For it, too, is the privilege, and should be the ambition, of men to chase opportunities that push their own boundaries in any niche of life, not only in the wild. Be it the field of academics, of enterprise, of relationships and love, of faith, of health, or any other human endeavour. By going out, getting lost, and taking risks in whatever we are doing, we find our limits.

Much like adventures, limits should not be thought of as distant and far off. They are, indeed, approachable in everyday life. They are the greatest approval you have received at work or the highest score at the end of a class term. They are the times when your nerves impede your ability to move forward and speak in front of a crowd or to a stranger. The steps before your mind convinces you that you can't run any further. The feeling that you should be honest before continuing to deceive because you don't think others will like the truth as much. Habits you cannot break and images of yourself you cannot discard.

Limits are everywhere, created either by yourself or others, telling you that you can't—or shouldn't—go any further. They tell you that what you're doing won't work or that it's too difficult. But what is the definition of difficult if not simply: This will take more practice than usual. Disregarding most of those in place for moral, protective, or legal reasons, we should prioritize meeting and interacting with our limits. By pushing toward them, we increase the probability that we will have the opportunity to face rejection and failure.

I know of no better teachers than rejection and failure. They are hard and concrete. Rejection after a sincere, well-intentioned effort has brought me more bliss than many successes.

I found myself quite affectionate toward a woman recently. We spoke and laughed about similar interests, and I was quickly able to see us together. And though she rejected my effort to court her beyond friendship, I walked away with nothing but joy. I expressed my endearment toward her through the belief that our relationship was something I valued and wanted to continue. I told her the truth and played my cards. I bear no regret nor any ill will and move on with a clear conscience. Most importantly, even though it was a fairly trivial rejection, I still feel that I learned about myself as a result. It gave me a greater understanding of the joy I receive from taking chances.

As the gravity of failures increases, so does the significance of the lessons to be learned from them. Two experiences of note come to mind. The first occurred during high school. I was a slightly above-average student. I didn't start to excel academically until late in my sophomore year of college. Upon graduation, I was not accepted to any of my top choice universities and watched as many of my friends went on to "better" schools. The memory of sitting in my English literature class after reading one specific college rejection email has been burned permanently into my prefrontal cortex. Seeing the reticent smiles of friends holding back their excitement after reading their acceptances, so as not to make me feel bad. Counting down the minutes until class ended. Knowing I would skip any remaining commitments that day for fear of tears. In my mind, I was the right choice; on paper, I wasn't. I thought I was "better" than my classmates, so how did they get into "better" colleges?

The second occurred during my first year of university when the coach of the D1 soccer team informed me they would not be taking me as a walk-on. My life revolved around this sport up until this point. My teams consisted of my closest friends. My conversations dwelled on recent professional games, highlight reels, and upcoming competitions. I dedicated my mornings to workouts and my afternoons to practice. And with a simple four-line text—that I admit still lives on my phone—I was no longer a competitive soccer player. Part of my identity that I had established for over a decade was gone in seconds.

I don't claim these experiences to be of jaw-dropping stature. But, at the time, they were exceedingly disappointing and difficult to accept. And they forced me to ask myself, "Why was I rejected?" The answer to this question is almost always simple. For me, the students who got into better universities and played collegiate soccer worked harder, more consistently, and for longer than I did. Of course, there are exceptions: the student who cheats his way through high school, whose parents donate millions, or whose connections allocate him a spot on a team. But the reality is that those are the exceptions and not the rule. And you should never live your life hoping to be the exception because *you are the rule*. I learned through these failures that one of the only reliable paths to success is through consistent, hard work.

Rejection—when you don't avoid it—will also make faults in your belief systems painfully obvious. If I had worked out at a young age with the same intensity as I did in high school, I would have had a stronger chance at becoming a collegiate soccer player. That was not obvious, unfortunately, until it was staring me dead in the eyes. And I would like to think that it was at this moment I became aware of reality. But, the truth is: I lied to myself, making up excuses for years about why I failed. This is because accepting reality would have meant accepting that I was not who I thought I was. And we will do anything, including lie to ourselves for years—maybe even our entire lives—to not change who we think we are.[52]

---

[52] Mark Manson, *The Subtle Art of Not Giving a F**k* (San Francisco: HarperOne, 2016). Though Mark Manson's commentary on what he calls "Manson's Law of Avoidance" is slightly different from what I say here, I think it is relevant and funny. Definitely worth a read.

Advance against your limits for exactly this reason; find the barriers that cause you to push back physically and mentally with the intention to change. "The wise man throws himself on the side of his assailants. It is more his interest than it is theirs to find his weak point."[53] Embrace different people's ideas and beliefs that might expand your mind. Explore for new adventures, even though they might make you feel weak. Seek out rejection because it will give you a greater understanding of reality. With that awareness comes the opportunity to learn lessons, sacrifice aspects of life that aren't working for you, change, and choose a path, which will make your reality better.

A byproduct of rejection and failure is the negative emotions generated in our minds. Reactions of contempt and resentment are not uncommon. This is an innate truth—one you cannot prevent. An important skill for dealing with these feelings is forgiveness. Forgiveness is merely the combination of acceptance and advancement. Acceptance of actions taken against someone, which offended or hurt that person, and advancement away from those feelings of soreness or pain. Though many actions deserve some form of retribution, realize that is only the physical aspect of the equation. Forgiveness in the real world is separate from forgiveness in our minds. We live in incredibly stimulating and overwhelming environments, which constantly drain away our reserves of energy. The more anger and contempt we harbor, the more energy we waste thinking of those people who have slighted us. And after spending all that energy on resentment, only a mere trickle remains to use for ourselves.

The worst person you can fail to forgive is yourself. I have spent a great deal of time clinging to the feelings of embarrassment that

---

[53] Ralph Waldo Emerson, "Compensation," in *Essays: First Series.* (Boston: J. Munroe and Company, 1847), 105.

followed the aforementioned rejections. Weeks of time spent over the past years, thinking not about *how* I could have done better—for the solutions were obvious—but instead only resenting that I *didn't* do better. But I forgave my 13-year-old self for not working out the way I did later, trying to catch up with my peers. Likewise, I forgave my high school and early collegiate self for my academics. At the time, I was busy learning from the dozens of other miscalculations and blunders that epitomize adolescence. With these self-pardons, I am now able to use that energy on more relevant matters. I did not attend an Ivy League school as an undergraduate nor did I make the cut as a collegiate soccer player. And because I forgave myself for those circumstances, I am a better man.

Opportunity, limits, rejection, failure, sacrifice, and forgiveness. All are branches which stem from a powerful trunk. This core is the privilege we have to experience one of life's greatest obligations: building mental resilience. The way our minds react to discomfort and pain—better known as suffering—is a test filled with meaning.

Everyone suffers in this life. Sure, if you're literate enough to read the words on this page, then there are many people in the world doing far worse than you. On this topic, there is unfortunately a passionate and well-intentioned, yet misguided and hostile, belief that so many thrust onto those around them. The claim that because others have pain, you cannot. There are numerous atrocities in the world. There is starvation and oppression and exploitation and unthinkable injustice. These are harsh realities that humans must make an effort to alleviate. And yet that truth does not, in any shape or form, discredit your own suffering. The pain of every individual is not mutually exclusive.

When I was 23 years old, ever a critic of surface-level discussion and a bit of an idiot, I carried on a work lunch conversation with a dozen people on this topic. The workplace is a capricious environment with many conversational pitfalls, and I would not recommend such heavy issues over dumplings. Several people participated, while the rest opted to remain a slightly uncomfortable audience. Though I forget the pretext, the hypothesis I claimed was—and still is—that you can always find meaning in pain and discomfort. If not in a way that will physically help you, such as by building muscle or flexibility, then in a way that will mentally help you. By building confidence or a better work ethic, by showing you places and people to avoid, by opening your mind to new ideas, or by giving you a taste of the real world. In response, I received humorous, pitying looks from my older, closer colleagues and a quite combative response from several not-as-close superiors. Their argument was, effectively, "Shut up kid. You don't know what pain is." This was followed maturely by, "What if you simply got punched in the face? Is that meaningful? Is the pain of childbirth meaningful if it could kill the mother, hmm?" At this moment, a well-respected colleague saved me, for I had no intention of backing down from my belief. She said that she refused anesthetization during the birth of her first child. She wanted to know what it would feel like. And then she said she was nervous. And then she said it was excruciating. And then she said it was real.

What does "real" mean here? It means not shying away from life. It means facing it head-on and demanding the truth from it. In the Nazi's Türkheim concentration camp outside of Dachau, where the prisoners were immersed in pain and suffering, the only escapes were avoiding reality or death itself. Remembering his time in this camp, Viktor Frankl asserts:

> ... *once the meaning of suffering had been revealed to us, we refused to minimize or alleviate the camp's tortures*

by ignoring them or harboring false illusions and enter-
taining artificial optimism. Suffering had become a task
on which we did not want to turn our backs. We had real-
ized its hidden opportunities for achievement ... [And]
there was no need to be ashamed of tears, for tears bore
witness that a man had the greatest of courage, the courage
to suffer. Only very few realized that.[54]

What meaning could possibly be found in this darkness? The answer is mental freedom. As David Goggins terms it: a "calloused, hard mind."[55] In any state of discomfort, from the smallest to the most intense, suffering brings about an opportunity to see the strength and the will of your mind. Do you recede from insults? Crumble under pressure? Avoid responsibility at work or in your own life? The solution to these weaknesses is the strengthening of your mind. To do that, one must face hardship with courage. That hardship might come in the form of a broken bone, a broken heart, or a broken will. Speaking to a friend in the concentration camps, Frankl asserted, "that someone looks down on each of us in difficult hours—a friend, a wife, somebody alive or dead, or a God—and he would not expect us to disappoint him. He would hope to find us suffering proudly, not miserably, knowing how to die."[56] To suffer proudly—which, in the case of a concentration camp prisoner, meant to face death proudly—is to confront the

---

[54] Viktor E. Frankl, Harold S. Kushner, and William J. Winslade, *Man's Search for Meaning* (Boston, MA: Beacon Press, 2014), 78.

[55] David Goggins, *Can't Hurt Me: Master Your Mind and Defy the Odds* (Lioncrest Publishing, 2018). The calloused, hard mind is one of David's most prominent messages, so it doesn't help to pinpoint one specific quote/time he talks about it. Just go read his book.

[56] Viktor E. Frankl, Harold S. Kushner, and William J. Winslade, *Man's Search for Meaning* (Boston, MA: Beacon Press, 2014), 83.

incredible burden of taking on full responsibility for the thoughts in your mind during your darkest hours. The man who endures pain and struggle with the perspective of growth emerges on the other side a different, stronger person.

This is one of the greatest reasons for people of any age to get into an activity that pushes their endurance limits. Any exercise that gets your heart rate up over an extended period of time will work. In my belief, this is why running is the most useful sport. It is one of the simplest paths to the realization that we are all pitifully awful when it comes to estimating our potential—because any nondisabled person is capable of going outside and running. Running until their thighs get heavy, their stomach aches with cramps, their breath quickens and shallows, their head gets light, calves tighten, shoulders close, lungs heave, and minds want to quit. Anyone can get there. They can do it anytime, for free, and most likely within 20 minutes. *That* is how simple it is.

You could put this essay away right now, go outside, and within minutes of hard running, be in enough pain and mental suffering that you will be at a breaking point for your mind: quit or continue? This is where you become a stronger person. Because when you choose to continue, you leap into unknown territory and pit yourself against your own mind. It wants you to stop, it tells you that you are in pain and that you don't have enough energy to continue. It tells you, "Sure, other people might do this; but, it's not your thing." With regard to your potential, screw your mind. Especially if you have a weak one.

This doesn't mean acting like an idiot. If you have a broken leg, don't run on it. But it does mean that if you're ending your run because it seems like you can't go any further, *it's because you've chosen to give up.* You let your mind walk all over you and tell you what your limits are instead of choosing to find them for yourself.

Chances are, if you let your mind overpower you, you also let your boss, colleagues, partner, family, or friends walk all over you, too. After all, if you can't face yourself in a moment of pressure, how could you face others?

This is why running helps so many people get out of slumps or fight depression. Not because they're able to run a couple (or a couple dozen) miles. But because in moments of struggle and self-doubt, when they find themselves in pain or they think they can't go on, they realize, "Wait. I've been here before. At mile 1 or at mile 10 or at mile 100, I thought I couldn't go on, *but I did*. If I was able to push past that limit, then maybe, just maybe, I can push through this one." All you need in these moments is *maybe*. Maybe means there's a chance. It means that this pain might be mental and will go away. It means that there might be a 2nd or 3rd or 4th or nth wind in your lungs. It means your will and your mind are toughening. Maybe means that you can take the pain and the suffering this world will inevitably give you and rise above it.

And then, when you have embraced that maybe, when you have challenged yourself to endure discomfort with courage, when you have realized that you are in control of your reactions, and when you have hardened your mind, you become resilient. This mental fortitude becomes the backbone of your life in all of your interactions. And when you die—when you stand before that self, who was supposed to teach you who you could be—you show him that his potential was just the start. You tenaciously stood up against the odds of life, willing to take as a lesson every hardship that came your way. You chose to take risks and embrace opportunities that pushed your potential. You sought out challenges which introduced you to struggle and suffering. And through that struggle and suffering you were introduced to yourself.

PRAY FOR LIGHTNING

Hawaii

December 31, 2019

I'm convinced Mother Nature is watching my trip. For two or three months now, I've had nonstop surf almost wherever I've gone. One of my best friends and his wonderful family let me sneak into their vacation for New Year's on the Big Island near Waikoloa. They told me that they've been coming here for a decade and have almost never seen surfable waves. It makes sense because the area faces north, so it's relatively protected from south swell in the summer. Yet it also has Maui directly to its north, probably protecting it from most winter surf.

However, an XXL northwest swell rolled through the day I arrived. It created waves with 30- to 40-foot faces on the north shores of Kauai and Oahu. With that much energy, there was plenty left to wrap around and send surf right at me. I can't imagine any better present I could have received to start off the Hawaiian leg of my trip.

I'm planning on buying a used board or two when I get to Oahu, so my surf travel companion for now is one of the wooden handplanes I made a while back. Together with a pair of fins, while the swell was rising, I swam out to a wave north of where we're staying. I watched some surfers earlier in the day to see how they got out; you have to maneuver around some fingers of the reef. While I was in the water, a group of three women paddled out. I chatted with them as the sets gradually got a bit bigger. It was a mother and daughter from the island with one of the daughter's visiting friends. Watching them, it was pretty obvious that the daughter's friend was not only a little scared, but at one point, after getting separated from the other two, also at risk of getting hurt. A couple more waves knocking her closer to a rocky segment of the shore, and she would be in a shallow, hazardous situation.

As she appeared to get more nervous and tired, it looked like she was making an effort to paddle back to shore. Without much success, I swam over and helped her. Pulling the board while swimming backward, I made some casual conversation to calm her down. All the while, I was praying to God that I didn't get spined in the back by an urchin as we weaved two or so feet above the reef below. I'd like to think that someone is at least *trying* to watch over you when you're doing nice things. Not to say that I'm protected while being kind, but I feel as if more shitty things occur in my life when I'm not making an effort to be a good person.

January 1, 2020

I swam out in Makaiwa Bay today. The surf was breaking in three spots. There was one hollow[57] peak at the end of a shallow reef, pitching onto jagged lava rock that poked out of the water in places. Probably best to leave that to the locals. A second

---

[57] Hollow means "barreling." This is where a wave heaves over itself and creates a cavity large enough for a surfer to fit in.

break 30 yards inside of that was peaking over a slightly deeper reef, but was crowded with people. The third only broke on larger sets further on the south side of the bay, near where a dive boat was anchored.

There's no chance I'll catch a wave body surfing in an area filled with stand-up paddleboarders and longboarders. With so much volume in their boards, they can catch waves long before they break, whereas bodysurfing requires you to catch them right as they pitch over. So I opted for the uncrowded third peak. It also seemed like a better option, considering some words from my older friend from Santa Cruz, who lived on the island for a couple years: "Big Island lava rock turn you to sashimi, brah." Noted. Opting for a break over slightly deeper water would probably mean a lower chance of having to say hello to some sharp Hawaiian reef on my second day out.

January 9, 2020

In Honolulu, I connected with the son of one of my mom's best childhood friends. She had moved to Oahu decades back, and her son had grown up on the island. The second time we met up, he invited me to come out with his friends for dinner followed by Dave & Buster's. D & B's in Honolulu on a Wednesday night is *not* what I expected. First off, it's three stories. A restaurant at the bottom, all the games and a couple bars on the second floor with an attached room dedicated as a *club*, and a rooftop bar. Secondly, it was filled with 20-somethings all dressed up trying to get laid. Not the relaxed "drink and try to win enough tickets to get a superball but actually end up with several of those stupid finger traps" environment I was personally familiar with—and kind of hoping for.

January 11, 2020

Met a cute girl in the water while I was surfing near Waikiki. Flirted briefly until I found out she was 15 years old. I rode the next wave straight to the sand.

January 23, 2020

I've surfed at Laniakea Beach a few times to get my bearings on the North Shore but decided instead to venture over toward Ehukai. I paddled out at head-high Log Cabins, another surf break in the area, and got absolutely *driiillled*. My first time getting cleaned up by a set of waves here, I actually had to get out of the water because I was so disoriented from it. It didn't help that my nerves were all over the place. I've heard nothing but crazy stories about the surf on the North Shore. You know that light feeling of butterflies in your stomach? I felt it the entire afternoon … in my arms. After regrouping on the sand from my first Hawaiian ocean-licking, I got back out in the water. The power of these waves takes some getting used to; they punch up fast and strong off the reef. I got caught off guard by this on the first few and ended up pin-dropping off the pop-up, falling from the top of the wave feet-first. I've heard scary stuff about the reef at Log Cabins but fortunately didn't have the opportunity yet to get any first-hand knowledge of it.

This was also my first time to check out Pipeline—an infamous surf break—from the water. Watching it from the side, the wave jacks up *so fast,* rising from a bump on the surface to a vertical wall in almost no time at all. It's absolutely wild. It's also interesting to see how the energy channels into the different reefs along the beach. While the waves at Log Cabins were around head high, they were easily three feet bigger at Rock Piles, another surf break maybe 150 feet away. Likewise, the breaks to the left and right of Pipeline were shoulder high on average, while Pipe remained consistently well-overhead. It's like the wave is sucking up the energy from the ones around it before breaking.

February 8, 2020

I hiked up toward Ka'ena Point, the northwest point of the island, a couple times during my stay in Oahu. The place is absolutely magical. During a massive northwest swell, easily three or four times larger than I'd ever paddled out into, I thought it would be cool to hike out there again to see what the waves and currents looked like. I brought a board just in case Mākaha, a famous town and surf break on the west side of Oahu, would be mortal-sized. But, upon walking onto the beach, I saw some locals paddling on huge boards into double-overhead-plus bombs.[58] I decided my lackluster ability on a 6' board would probably get me killed. Opting for life, I drove on and went for a hike—and what I saw *defied* imagination.

Scanning the water, between sets of massive hills rolling from the north, exploding two or three stories off the rocks, among a mess of currents looking like they were going in every direction, I saw this *wave*. Everything else I saw for a half hour was chaos— turbulent mountains of swell moving with no rhyme or reason— except for this one random freak-of-nature occurrence. Maybe the stars had aligned because this colossal, gorgeous, teal blue steam train of death moved rapidly along the point. It even accelerated as it started to break right down the line, perfectly parallel to shore. Absolutely unsurfable, sure, but mesmerizing. Like in *The Endless Summer's* Cape Saint Francis scene, where they ride a perfect head-high wave down what appears to be hundreds of yards. Except in this case the wave appeared to be 17 times overhead, rolling for miles, and on PCP. Only in nature do you find events with such a

---

[58] "Bombs" are large waves. Pronounced, "Dude, that's a booooooooomb!!"

balance of unbelievable terror and true beauty. Maybe things like this are Mother Nature's way of reminding us that, though we can transplant organs and modify our genetics, she's still in charge.

February 9, 2020

I am such an idiot. This is easily one of the dumbest things I've done so far on this trip. Ala Moana Beach Park has some fun surf, even with small swells. To get to it, you paddle out from the beach across the lagoon and then maneuver through the shallow reef. Past that, it gets slightly deeper and there are a couple of fun surf breaks. It's quite cool because the almost random shape of the reef underneath redirects the swell in all sorts of directions, some waves making 90-degree turns over maybe 20 yards. It seems random, but there's always a pattern to be found.

The reef has several ways to get across. There's a deeper segment you can paddle over on the west side, a route you can walk across near the middle, and then a maze of shallow reef you can maneuver around on your belly at high tide on the east. It doesn't take a genius to find them—just follow the locals. Little mister dipshit over here (me), however, decides that after a handful of sessions, he knows where to go and has it aaalllll on lock. Ten minutes later, I'm dancing on a not-super-sharp-but-sharp-enough reef in about six inches of water. It was one of the most frustratingly embarrassing situations I've experienced. Frustrating because it was 100 percent avoidable and already painful, disregarding what was to come. Embarrassing because there were people 200 feet on either side of me walking or paddling over the reef where you're *supposed* to go. Even a surf school group was walking by me, and that hit my ego hard.

Anyway, I'm sidestepping what appear to be hundreds of silver-dollar sized urchins, trying to avoid the more-obvious edges of the reef, holding a nine-foot longboard over my head. Already a bummer situation, pissed off at myself and the world, the wind would blow over the surface every 30 seconds, creating a rippled texture that prevented me from seeing through it. Many steps were preceded by the thought, "Well, it didn't look like there was an urchin there ..." Like walking on a minefield filled with mines that kept showing themselves and then disappearing. Granted these mines wouldn't kill you, but they'd probably make you regret getting out of bed that day. With every stride, a bit of the coral underneath collapsed (sorry, world), slightly cushioning my step. But juuuuust enough would break off, pierce the skin, and lodge in my foot.

About halfway across the reef to the waves, I looked around and realized that I had calculated probably the worst—meaning longest—possible route. After 25 minutes of waltzing with the reef, wishing that a tidal wave would come and wash me back to land or a lightning bolt would come out of the cloudless blue sky and kill me, I finally made it to deeper water. While paddling out, I was greeted by—I swear—*maybe* shin-high waves. All that stupidity and pain for awful surf. I mean, I knew it wasn't going to be great, but from the shore it didn't look *this* bad. So I caught four or five tiny waves over an extremely shallow reef (generally, the smaller the wave the shallower the water needed for it to break), and then decided it would be best to go in and clean up my feet. This wasn't worth infection in the dozens of cuts I probably had. Thankfully, I avoided all the urchins, and upon return to shore (through one of the actual places to paddle out), I realized that the extreme calluses I had built up over the past years had prevented 90 percent of the cuts from piercing deep enough to bleed and get infected. Still, with no Kiani[59] to ride over on her horse and put aloe on my wounds, I spent the rest of the afternoon tweezing bits of rock, reef, and shell out of my feet. Well done, bud.

---

[59] A reference to a character in the surfing cult classic movie, *North Shore.*

RESPONSIBILITY

Freedom is but the negative aspect of the whole phenomenon whose positive aspect is responsibleness.

— Viktor Frankl,
Man's Search for Meaning

Free men will only remain independent so long as they take responsibility for their freedom. Every time a man makes a decision, reacts to his environment, or even takes a step, he must hold himself accountable for his actions. His ability to reach his potential relies on this decision to always answer for his conduct. Each and every one of us has an untapped well of potential, waiting to be drawn from. Potential, however, is a choice. Do you tempt fate by taking the easy, weak route? Or do you look only toward the path that will better you? Greatness seeks goodness. Peeking down each road and finding the trials that await. Not seeking out the most difficult, but rather the most moral and meaningful one. And by choosing to endure the difficulties that might come from traveling this worthwhile road, greatness accepts responsibility for its future.

It is obvious he who looks beyond the horizon, and he who is satisfied with the shore. Look around you. You will see which of your peers recognize that they have great potential. The demeanor of those who reach beyond their current capability emanates a gentle calmness. Not necessarily through their actions, but through their condition. It is the composure of one who endeavors. They might not know what their future holds, nor what their potential looks like, but they know they will always follow the path that they believe pushes them forward.

A captain, beset and forced off course by a violent storm, shifts his sails according to the stars after the winds have ceased. He trusts that they will lead him and his companions on the correct path. And though he will never say it, he *is* afraid that they won't. He is frightened that his course has deviated too far and that his life and those of his crew are at risk. Regardless of this unease, he takes command and follows his knowledge of the luminescent heavens. Trusting that they will guide him more steadfastly than the current of the ocean and winds themselves.

It is unlikely you will manifest your potential exactly. But you may always decide that your current future is not where you want to go. David Goggins experienced a brutal adolescence; he later personally described himself as "the poster child of at-risk youth." At 23, he was obese, in a failing relationship, and stuck in a dead-end job. He was in a dark place, one that most will never be able to imagine, yet he "knew that if [he] continued to surrender to [his] fear and [his] feelings of inadequacy, [he] would be allowing them to dictate [his] future forever."[60] No matter where one falls on the spectrum of disappointment, they still have the opportunity to change course. The ability to adjust direction lies in the capacity to honestly assess one's current state and see which options are available. Then, he or she must weigh

---

[60] David Goggins, *Can't Hurt Me: Master Your Mind and Defy the Odds* (Lioncrest Publishing, 2018), 93.

those options, judging them not by the reward that would follow, but by their moral worth.

Which options will best deliver the good in you to the world? Which of them will instead bring out the worst? Goggins had several choices. He could let his negative thoughts and emotions drive him toward inadequacy, toward the evil that is the destruction of self. Or, he could choose good. He knew his only positive course was to instead "try [and] find power in the emotions that had laid [him] low," and, "harness and use them to empower [him] to rise up."[61] It is evident that such a decision leads to a far more difficult existence, one with an inundation of difficult trials and challenges. Why choose this? Why choose a more burdensome life without any promise of success? One evident reason is this: By choosing to aim for your potential, it will not *only* benefit you, but will undoubtedly make a positive impact on those around you as well. In Goggins' case, this meant the lives of his friends and future family, the men he recruited to the Navy Seals, and the people he inspired with his memoir. His reach and influence were greater because he chose to aim toward his potential. He chose to explore and discover his best self.

What wonderful inspiration to seek excellence! You know what the here and now feels like—what you've always gotten and what you're convinced you will always get. But out there? Where your potential lies? It is unimaginable, for how could one understand his potential until he has lived it? Your own story is the greatest epic yet to be written. What an adventure it can be to unveil the secrets that each page of your potential offers! Which pages will have creased corners, where you might look back and

---

[61] Goggins, *Can't Hurt Me*, 93.

see the exciting twists and turns and the good you have done through your actions?

Such great effort not only provides for yourself, but also for your family, your friends, and even the community at large. Living on the verge of your potential will turn your memoir into the hero's adventure, where you, the champion, will compel its readers to live improved lives. This hero—this man of courage—will be able to support the people he loves more than he is capable of doing now. Whether that be financially, emotionally, intellectually, or in any other context, the better you become, the better off those around you become, too. In this connected era, there is no action that does not affect another indirectly. And in an existence where every individual advances toward the best version of themselves, the positive influence would be immeasurable.

This description of acquiring one's potential makes light of the process, as if it is as easy as aiming and shooting in a different direction. But in reality, the work required to make such life changes and to realize such possibilities cannot be put into words on a page. Any attempt to do so would trivialize it.

The outset of this growth might be the most difficult, even if not the most arduous. To start changing oneself, a person must take on the incredible burden of assuming accountability for their reaction to all that occurs in their lives. To all the mistakes you have made, all the errors of your ways, all the rejections you have endured, everything that makes you discontented—big, small, unimportant, or awful. It is entirely your responsibility to decide how you will react to all of it.

There is a likely chance that many of these predicaments are your own justifications for why you cannot continue. The walls you falsely believe are impenetrable were actually built *by you*. You are preventing yourself from reaching your potential because you're scared of what you might do. You're scared of being great. Maybe it's because you're scared of failure. Maybe it's because you're scared of change. Maybe you don't believe that you deserve it. Whatever the reason, know the following to be impeccably true: No one but you is capable of breaking down the walls which obstruct you. Furthermore, you are the only one whose responsibility it is to even try.

There are three common rejections to this philosophy. The first being that it seems unfair. And at times it certainly may be. But, it appears to me that by taking responsibility, you gain an impression of control. In the face of adversity, in the face of disappointment, in the face of any challenge, you gain a sense of command. When you insist that you would like to help fix a current issue, whether it was your fault or not, you take a stance that is conducive to progress. You let the world rest on your shoulders, even if briefly uncomfortable, and view it with a perspective of authority. You let colleagues and companions know that you not only take responsibility for the situation, you demand it. Because that is your best chance at making real progress.

Second comes via a desire for balance. This is a view that erroneously equates personal accountability with productivity. Being responsible for the way you react to the world does not require working ad nauseam nor needing more wealth or influence than you have. It is not about late nights at the office; it is about your actions while you are there. Simply put, when faced with decisions, do you, or do you not, make the ones that you honestly believe should be made?

Lastly, there are injustices, which others have taken against you, that are so unfair that they prevent you from acting rightly. *Of course* there are injustices in the world. History has many dark, unspeakable moments of evil. This is why experiences disclosed by those who have lived through such times are invaluable. Taking this theory of accountability to the extreme, to the death and labor camps of Auschwitz-Birkenau and Türkheim, among others, Viktor Frankl teaches us that even in the most unbelievable oppression, all men can claim responsibility for their actions. He does not waver in *Man's Search for Meaning* on his view that "man is not fully conditioned and determined but rather determines himself whether he gives into conditions or stands up," to injustices.[62]

You are an individual, capable of original thought and bold expression. But only if *you* "decide what [your] existence will be," if *you* decide "what [you] will become in the next moment."[63] It is entirely up to you how you establish yourself in the face of adversity. No individual or group can take away your ability to control your mental reaction to *any* situation. If you let anyone or anything decide how you will react to life—your upbringing, your genetics, your religion, your politics, or your friends—then you have deliberately forfeited the most foundational aspect of your humanity.

Things fall apart. You will get hurt. You will be heartbroken. You will get fired, treated unfairly, or rejected. But relinquishing control over your mind is your own failing; "the power men possess to annoy [you, you] give to them by weak curiosity. No man can come near [you] but through [your] act."[64] It is entirely at your discretion to let others affect you. And why should anyone deserve the right to agitate you? Is your mind not important enough to keep charge over? Every time something unfortunate happens,

---

[62] Viktor E. Frankl, Harold S. Kushner, and William J. Winslade, *Man's Search for Meaning* (Boston, MA: Beacon Press, 2014), 131.

[63] Frankl, *Man's Search for Meaning*, 131.

[64] Ralph Waldo Emerson, "Self-Reliance," in *Essays: First Series* (Boston: J. Munroe and Company, 1847), 63.

it grants you the privilege to exert your control over yourself in a new, adverse situation! Every time you get pushed down, you receive the *gift* of being able *to stand back up*. It may not have started with you, but it can end with you, if you choose strength and accountability over weakness.

Not all efforts can be successful, however. In failing to instill a habit or in a personal defeat, you may be overcome with remorse. You may wake up in the mornings with guilt or shame from dishonest actions. This is life. This is simply the wonderful opportunity to appreciate that you have perceived something that you want to change. Do not be discouraged; instead, revel in the fact that you are aware. Know that you will continue to make mistakes, but with each conscious decision to rectify or learn from them, you will cement such changes in your character.

Regardless of success or failure, all our decisions show what we have to offer—in a moral sense. When faced with a problem, one will develop many options as to how they might proceed. Some lead to a positive result, some to a negative one. The surface level content of these results has deeper, implicit significance. Your actions are an extension of you, and any harm done by them is harm done by you. If you act in a petty or immoral way, you deliver your own pettiness and immorality into the world.

There is no need to be apprehensive in realizing that you are capable of wickedness. All humans have meanness within; all humans are capable of unspeakable acts. The extermination camps, the gulags, slave trade—*crimes against humanity*—were enacted by humans with nearly the same genetic code as you, were they not? Dark shadows, however, can still be conceived by radiant light. See which of your actions might instead manifest the greatest blessings you have to offer. This is the spectrum of moral possibility. All your actions exist somewhere on it, leading you toward brightness or darkness. Without this frame of reference, you may naively assume your intentions are righteous when they are not. Using the context of your moral capabilities, you create a scale upon which each action can be judged virtuous or vicious.

By knowing the most wicked thoughts and actions you are capable of, by knowing the full range of ethical opportunity, you amass remarkable self-authority. Instead of merely being your best self by chance, you take control of your action's outcome. You now may be impeccable by conscious choice, not out of ignorance for the other options. This consideration to bear your light instead of your darkness is to take complete responsibility for yourself. I wrote the following to a friend on this theme:

> *There are two groups of people: those that accept their environment as fact and those that accept it as their perception of fact. The prior interprets the world with limited control while the latter interprets it with complete control. Not of its outcome but of its impact on them. Every action taken here on earth is only as important as you decide it is. Our human experience, from how our memories are encoded to how we act on them, is not driven by what actually occurred. Instead it is only driven by what we perceive to have occurred. It's common for people to talk about being "responsible for our actions," but maybe we should be talking about being "responsible for our perceptions." Change the light with which you see the world from anger or sadness to joy or gratefulness and you will physically remember the same actions differently ... and respond to them accordingly.*

Anthony Ray Hinton was wrongly convicted of two murders and held captive on death row for almost three decades.

When freed, his transgressors gave no apology nor assistance in his transition to a present day that had left him behind. How could anyone blame a man, to whom such evil was done, if he were to only feel impassioned resentment for those who incarcerated him? But that isn't what happened. He understood that his perception—his reaction—was not only under his control, but *would determine how he would live the rest of his days.* He chose to be accountable for his attitude, knowing that even though they had taken 30 years of his life, "what joy [he has now, he] cannot afford to give to them."[65] Doing so would be to *choose* anger. Let this wonderful man's words resound forevermore in your mind: "How can I smile when I am full of hate?"[66] How you see the world changes *everything*. It can turn anger into appreciation, find love within hate, and make the impossible possible. This is because your actions, and therefore your very being, stem from how you interpret your environment and the events which occur in it.

This is all about *you*. It does not mean that awful actions do not reflect the awful character of another person. You can decide to not associate with a man who has hurt you without being angry at him. And if they really have hurt you, then it would be wise not to keep them in your life. Do not turn the other way when faced with atrocities; resolutely move forward, leaving such negativity in your past. It is, afterall, your choice to see the path back to or away from them. I am partial to Edward Abbey's address

[65] Anthony Ray Hinton, "Life After Death Row," interview by Scott Pelley, *60 Minutes*, CBS News, January 10, 2016. https://www.cbsnews.com/news/60-minutes-life-after-death-row-exoneration/. I first read about this story in The Book of Joy: Lasting Happiness in a Changing World by Dalai Lama XIV, Desmond Tutu, and Douglas Abrams. I highly recommend reading this book or listening to the audiobook..
[66] Hinton, interview.

of this capability for us to perceive such outlooks from the same environment:

> *There are inevitable pious Midwesterners who climb a mile and a half under the desert sun to view Delicate Arch and find only God ... and the equally inevitable students of geology who look at the arch and see only Lyell and the uniformity of nature. You may therefore find proof for or against His existence. Suit yourself. You may see a symbol, a sign, a fact, a thing, without meaning or a meaning which includes all things.*[67]

A former girlfriend and I were looking out over a city atop a nearby ridgeline. For several minutes we sat, taking in the view, the orange sun setting over the distant mountains. Cars swirled up the switchbacks low on the hill. Darkness crept from the far side of the valley, quietly approaching as the lights of the buildings below began to shimmer cheerfully. She asked me what I saw and thought of the scene. I told her of the wonderful sunset, the feeling of the wind that rustled the grasses and trees, and of my appreciation for the stars that were coming out and starting to blanket the sky. In response, she told me that she enjoyed the city and suburb lights, picturing the million people below us and all that was going on at that very moment. The smiles, the dinners, the love, the arguments, the shows, everything we could imagine—even if we could not see it directly—was happening right in front of us.

Our views were distinctly different, yet both perfectly true. We were looking at the exact same scene and perceiving *entirely* different pictures. As mentioned in the above Abbey quote, the

---

[67] Edward Abbey, *Desert Solitaire* (New York: Touchstone, 1990), 36.

christian and the geologist are able to see a rock arch in the desert as a symbol "without meaning or a meaning which includes all things." Similarly, my ignorance of the scene below me was due to my preference for the stars. Her ignorance of the scene above was due to her preference for the people. Find what you will in life, see what you will in life, perceive what you will in life. *Simply know that what you experience is entirely your choice.*

Following this theme, one product of our perceptions is our expectations. When you see the world one way, you may expect it to always be that way, or you might expect certain things to happen, just because you think they should. This isn't inherently bad. In the form of visualization, expectations can help someone build a scaffolding upon which they will implement a process. They can help a person recreate themselves. They can also be useful in setting standards. There is nothing wrong with expecting a woman to be kind; that is a great standard to expect of someone you are thinking about dating.

Where this goes wrong—where expectations hinder us instead of help us—is when they become too precise. Projecting exacted imagination onto reality steals its opportunities to infatuate the mind. If you decide what actions a kind woman must carry out, then you will always be disappointed. For she will never fulfill your expectations. You will be so disappointed, in fact, that you will not be able to see her *real* gestures of kindness, which she does provide.

A very tough niche of expectations are those that deal with success. You dream of what success will look like. In your head you see the view from your corner office, you choose the title of your position and the suit or dress you will be wearing. You know every little detail, what it looks like, what it sounds like, what it tastes like, what it costs, when it will happen, why it will happen, and—worst of all—what it will *feel* like. But it has not happened yet. You pray to a false image. You have robbed yourself of the present. The views, the tastes, the feelings, they will all be different than you imagined—than you *expected*. In reality, the success will be far greater, with so much detail that could never have been imagined. Yet in your mind, it will be hollow. With your vision narrowed, you choose to limit your ability to perceive reality. You preclude yourself from ever having the opportunity to feel the wonder—the awe—of the truth. Do not miss out on all that the present has to offer or on the pride in yourself, which you worked so hard for, by obscuring yourself with fantasy.

When I think of people who embody this ability to take responsibility for their view of the world and their resulting actions, there are a select few that come to mind. In my life so far, these empathetic mentors took the form of soccer coaches, family friends, and graduation speakers. They appear to share a similar spirit—one that I was not able to define for a long time. Rereading Emerson's *Self-Reliance*, I realized that he had perfectly coined a term for these men and women I looked up to. Each embodies his commentary of the "self-helping man."

Seek out the independent soul. If your vision can pick him out, you have found the secret to the greatest riches. You have found the secret to moral wealth. Our hero who is "welcome evermore to gods and men is the self-helping man. For him all doors are flung wide: all tongues greet, all honors crown, all eyes follow with desire."[68] Why do we care so greatly about this man? Why do we love him? Why do we "solicitously and apologetically caress and celebrate him?"[69] Why does it seem as

---

[68] Ralph Waldo Emerson, "Self-Reliance," in *Essays: First Series* (Boston: J. Munroe and Company, 1847), 69.

[69] Emerson, *Essays*, 69.

if he has a celestial immunity from the struggles, which most others feel ingrained in their everyday life? Simple. It is because he does not need you.

What power is this independence that compels us to imbibe so heavily from the grail of the self-helping man's actions? "The unstable estimates of men crowd to him whose mind is filled with a truth, as the heaped waves of the Atlantic follow the moon."[70] I speculate that this insincere attending is driven not out of compassion but out of scorn. The common man covets the confidence this champion exudes and the faith he holds in himself. He desires the independent soul's regard because he knows that such attention only befalls legitimately worthy people and things. Lastly, however convoluted it may be, the common man wants to see the self-helping man fail. He wants him to be dependent, on his knees, begging for help. Most do not want to see another who delineates so much that they cannot see in themselves.

Any "man passes for that he is worth. What he is engraves itself on his face, on his form, on his fortunes, in letters of light."[71] The independent of mind cannot be turned away by misfortune. Fire him, and he will create work with his own hands. Starve him, and he will provide for himself with spade and trowel. Steal from him, and he will rebuild his fortune without a hint of vengeance. The only way to connect with him is by becoming him. For you, too, could become the self-helping man—the independent soul. You, too, could wake up before the aurora with a collected, calm, and faithful mind. The only way to conquer the self-serving is to

[70] Ralph Waldo Emerson, "The American Scholar," *Essays* (New York: Charles E. Merrill & Co., 1907) para. 33.

[71] Ralph Waldo Emerson, "Spiritual Laws," in *Essays: First Series* (Boston: J. Munroe and Company, 1847), 142.

relinquish any want of power over them. Power over yourself is far more compelling.

The best road to this independence is the path paved with your values. But it is not enough to view the road, you must travel it. "Good thoughts are no better than good dreams, unless they be executed!"[72] Actions aligned with your character build confidence. Words spoken against immorality and tyranny bolster determination. For those who do not speak will never be heard. But men who communicate their character clearly every day find an authority in themselves that obviates any need for control over others. Even amongst their enemies, they will only feel openness. They are not controlled by hate or jealousy and therefore can consciously decide to move forward without them.

Think of someone who has influenced you through their self-reliant action and independence. Why do they illustrate greatness to you? Is it because of the potential that they had when they were young? No, it is because of the experiences they collected as they lived. It is because they took their map and their compass, and they *used* them. They left the comfort of their home and found a life worth living. When they look at their youth, they will resound: "Instead of possibilities, I have realities in my past, not only the reality of work done and of love loved, but of suffering bravely suffered."[73] You look up to such people not because of how great they could be, but because of how great they *became*.

Those who believe they understand the trials of another are foolish. You did not experience what they experienced and may

---

[72] Ralph Waldo Emerson, *Nature* (Boston & Cambridge: James Munroe and Company, 1849), Chapter V: Language, para. 3.
[73] Viktor E. Frankl, Harold S. Kushner, and William J. Winslade, *Man's Search for Meaning* (Boston, MA: Beacon Press, 2014), 121.

not lay any claim to their knowledge. When you are to pass history to your children, will you only have stories from other great men? Or will you have stories from your own life? Find the work *you* will toil, the love that *you* will cherish, the suffering that *you* will bravely endure.

This is the marvelous power of the memoir and the biography. Great, independent people lived their lives to be themselves. The real gift they give you is the realization that you, too, can be yourself. Not by imitating their actions, but by finding your own novel course. Persist in the direction of your own compass; create your own original story. Let it then be with excitement—accompanying the mind's symphony, building with bravado—that you listen to this affirmation of Emerson:

> *Know then that the world exists for you. For you is the phenomenon perfect. What we are, that only we can see. All that Adam had, all that Caesar could, you have and can do. Adam called his house, heaven and earth; Caesar called his house, Rome; you perhaps call yours, a cobbler's trade; a hundred acres of ploughed land; or a scholar's garret. Yet line for line and point for point your dominion is as great as theirs, though without fine names. Build, therefore, your own world. As fast as you conform your life to the pure idea in your mind, that will unfold its great proportions.[74]*

It is not the grandeur of your claim, for already we are at capacity with conquerors. Instead, it is simply how you decide to assert

---

[74] Ralph Waldo Emerson, *Nature* (Boston & Cambridge: James Munroe and Company, 1849), Chapter VIII: Prospects, para. 17.

your own free will. Extricate yourself from the ill-fitting shackles placed on your hands by your pursuit of the dreams of others. Free yourself from the fantasy that you must imitate your heroes. You exist in a world that has been given wholly to you. Will you act with integrity because you see others doing it, or will you walk proudly on the path of rectitude out of your own volition?

Viktor Frankl found that even in the face of unprecedented evil, "in the concentration camps, for example," man still draws his own claim. "We watched and witnessed some of our comrades behave like swine while others behaved like saints. **Man has both potentialities within himself, which one is actualized depends on decisions, but not on conditions.**"[75] Stand your ground knowing that even if it is to be ripped away from under your feet, the will of your mind can never be stolen. Find the mindset that sees opportunity in all obstacles, that seeks to support itself against any uncertainty.

The significance of your life's story will be the product of whatever mindset you upheld throughout it. The common man adapts a weak ethos and buries his will. Yet the moment he chooses to take accountability for his actions, he grasps at the spade and rediscovers the opportunity for change. He again finds his individuality. He finds the privilege of a life uniquely lived.

He requests responsibility from himself for the good or the evil that he delivers. Consequently, he decides that the duty of making the world better falls on him. As it falls on you. As it falls on me. He finds meaning by acting and experiencing and perceiving prudently. And the rewards he may reap become inconsequential, for his auspicious actions indemnify him. He lives with the truth, he drives a life of action, and so he becomes a *man of action*.

---

[75] Viktor E. Frankl, Harold S. Kushner, and William J. Winslade, Man's Search for Meaning (Boston, MA: Beacon Press, 2014), 134. My formatting.

YOU GOTTA GET STUNG
TO FIND OUT

Leaving Hawaii, Reaching Australia

February 11, 2020

One of my initial apprehensions about Hawaii was the locals. Not on land, but in the water while surfing. Everyone's heard stories of angry locals at any popular surf break. But Hawaii tends to have a pretty heavy reputation for this. From my experience in California, people *can* be friendly, but in general, if you're not one of the crew at a given spot or if it's not an older group, few people are going to go out of their way to say hello. And even though I'm a pretty friendly dude, finding conversation wherever I go, I still find tons of people up and down the coast who are completely silent in the water. I'm all for grunting and yelling and hassling for waves when they're there and good. But a group of 15 guys sitting in the beautiful ocean, all angry over two-foot tall slop and not saying anything to each other, bewilders me. And in my head, California is a land of generally friendly people, so hearing that Hawaii was more tense than this was a bit intimidating.

With that said, I have never in my life met so many wonderful and kind people as I have so far while surfing in Hawaii.

171

I've surfed all over Oahu at dozens of different breaks. And each time I paddle into the water with a smile and say hello, I've been greeted in turn with aloha. Let's be clear here, though—there are some biiiiig, tatted, *intimidating* looking guys in the water out here. But as the saying goes, "if you can bite, you generally don't have to." My Hawaiian rule of thumb has become: the gnarlier a dude looks, the bigger his smile. Not like I was planning on disrespecting these guys in the first place, though; I do value my life.

For example, while paddling out into some fun-sized surf at Haleiwa, a surf break on the North Shore, this *behemoth*, covered in tattoos, who looked like he could snap a person in half, dropped into a wave. Honestly, it was surprising that the ocean was even supporting this beast of a man. My initial thought was that I wouldn't even glance in his general vicinity, let alone at a wave he was planning to surf. But when he paddled back out to the lineup after his wave, he was the first one to swim by and smile at me.

Surfing on the West Side, I was even more cautious because it's known as the "local" side of the island. Pitbulls in the back of each pickup act as car alarms. In the water, I was trying to say hello to three pretty heavyset guys, who were obviously local, and managed to squeak, "Hey, you guys from here? This place is wicked beautiful." In response, all three started to laugh. The one at the peak bellowed, "Ahaha haole,[76] you even gotta ask that brah?!?" Then, for the next two hours, we exchanged a couple laughs, and they nodded me into some awesome waves.

The treatment of Hawaii and its citizens since its controversial annexation and takeover in the late 19th century is quite

---

[76] Hawaiian word for foreigner, usually white. It's not a derogatory term ... unless it's being used as one. Understood?

sad. While an incredibly complex issue, the results of this can be seen via the displacement of natives onto certain parts of the islands and the poverty, homelessness, and incarceration rates. Hawaiians have endured a tough hundred-plus years. From my half-dozen or so trips out here and these brief two months, however, it seems pretty clear that nearly everything in Hawaii—in the water and out of it—is about respect, regardless of the history. Obviously there's a spectrum everywhere, and you're going to find criminals and bad people out here, too. But as a whole, Hawaiians are the most respectful and friendly group I've ever personally met. And that has made the sport of surfing so much more fun for me.

February 14, 2020

After half a week of pumping surf, I went through a brutal couple of days. The post-surf-bender depression phenomenon is an interesting one. I imagine it is as close as someone can get to clinical depression without having it. It's also one that I believe I have an interesting perspective on, being that I didn't start surfing consistently until I was 19 or so. It's an adrenaline-heavy sport, like skiing and snowboarding, but with a few differences. When skiing, besides maybe in whiteout or extremely steep conditions, there's almost always time for rest or thought before a certain section if you need it. That luxury doesn't exist in the ocean; there is no opportunity to freeze the sea and opt out. If there's a freak set of waves coming to clean everyone up, chances are you're about to get pounded.

I've done a range of endurance activities in my life that entail some adrenaline—competitive soccer, Half Ironmans, open-water swims, 20-25+ mile and 10,000+ vertical foot day hikes, etc. But nothing has *ever* made me feel so low as the days after a multi-day surf-bender. Three or four days in a row in big surf,[77] getting fried from the sun, competing with other people for waves, adrenaline constantly surging. Those other activities I mentioned wore me out physically—some mentally as well. But surfing wears me out even more than that. Every muscle tired, my brain fried, and probably every hormone level off balance. Complete, utter exhaustion.

While I doubt it's possible for anyone to become completely tolerant to this, I could imagine that people who grew up surfing can probably better handle the surges of adrenaline. For me, I had never felt anything like this. The first time I went into one of these lows I couldn't even comprehend what was going on. Eating lunch in Ojai, southern California, an uncomfortable feeling swept over me that I needed to be in my bed. Feeling *something* coming, not knowing what, but with the understanding that I needed calories and water, I scarfed down everything in sight and proceeded to get back to my van. Then I spent the next several hours lying face up staring at the ceiling. Not sore, but depleted. I can't really describe it; I felt so tired that I didn't even have the energy to sleep. I just lay there, debilitated. At first I thought something bad was happening to me, and being alone, it felt scary. A bit of anxiety that took some calm breathing to relax. But while resting there, I realized that I had been in threatening, cold surf for the entirety of the past several days, frying under the sun. And now, with the first opportunity for my adrenaline levels to go back to normal after multiple days (excluding sleep of course), my body clearly understood that it

---

[77] Because everyone gets used to larger waves as they progress, "big" in this context is strictly relative to the surfer's ability and experience. I doubt the objective size matters as far as your adrenal response is concerned.

was not under attack anymore. It was "safe" again, and it set out to repair, well, everything, I guess.

It gives me an even better perspective on the consistently troubled lives of professional surfers or, really, competitive athletes in general. Battling constant, huge swings of emotion. Super-highs falling to super-lows. Trying to deal with them while competing with others who are struggling with those same demons. All under a spotlight of screaming fans. Imagine being in this exhausted state and having to compete over and over again, with your rival on the opposite end of the spectrum. Being physically, mentally, and hormonally exhausted and looking into the eyes of your competitor who is riding a tidal wave of dopamine.

February 15, 2020

My friends who were letting me stay at their apartment were coming back on February 24th. I was looking online for cheap flights to somewhere in Oceania, but every flight for the next 30 days to go almost anywhere was $600+. Except for one flight: $205 to Sydney, Australia, on February 24th. Couldn't be a coincidence.

February 22, 2020

I had one of the most perfect days of the entire trip so far. Unbelievably fun surf at Rock Piles all day on the North Shore. Crystal clear blue skies and water. Wonderful, positive atmosphere. A captivating sunset over Rocky Point. Why on earth would I consciously choose to leave this? No way. I'm coming back. Soon.

February 25, 2020

In the Honolulu airport, there were easily a thousand people waiting for security, almost all checking into flights for Southeast

Asia. Every single one of them was wearing a mask over their face because of this whole coronavirus ordeal. To be fair, I've never felt like an airport has ever been cleaner than when everyone else's face is covered. Plus, I think it's comical to see people in face masks touching literally every door handle, table, and wall with their bare hands. Nice try, guys.

February 27, 2020

My first day in Australia, I took the ferry over to Manly Beach. The surf was alright, and I thought jumping in would be a great way to christen this leg of the trip. I went to a local shop to rent a board but remembered that Australia has deadly jellyfish, something we don't have in California. When I asked the guy behind the counter about them, he replied with the most Australian response I could imagine:

> "Oh, the stingas down here? No worries about them unless you're allergic!"
> "Yeah man, I have no clue if I'm allergic or not."
> "Oh? Well ya gotta get stung to find out, mate!"

Tough to argue with that logic.

February 28, 2020

Took the train down to Wollongong, two hours south of Sydney, to meet up with a professor I connected with online. He does research on surfboards and fins, which I thought sounded interesting, mixing business with pleasure in a cool way. We had a chat, and he showed me his laboratory. The labs I worked in at my previous job had extremely sensitive equipment worth hundreds of thousands of dollars. This one had a hundred surfboards stacked on the walls, and this professor had done "research" surfing in the Mentawais, an island chain in Indonesia. Not sure which is cooler, but I'm certainly leaning toward the latter.

March 2, 2020

I was talking about Australian spiders with a guy in my hostel on Bondi Beach. He told me that a while ago he left his board shorts to dry on a rack in his friend's house. While he was letting them dry, a huntsman spider decided that it would be a wonderful place to take a quick rest. Huntsman spiders aren't poisonous and rarely bite. *However,* they can easily be the size of your palm, move extremely fast, are furry, and grip onto nearly anything. Oh, did I mention they're skittish and can JUMP? Yeah. Apparently, the whole "click your shoes and check under your sheets before going to bed" thing is not an exaggeration here.

PURPOSE

*"Ille hic es Raphael timuit quo sospite vinci rerum
magna parens et morient mori."*
*"Here lies Raphael, by whom Nature feared to be
outdone while he lived, and when he died,
feared that she herself would die."*[78]

— Pope Gregorio XVI

Place a new log upon the slowly fading embers of the hearth. Small wisps of fire flare up, circumventing and welcoming the newcomer. Quickly, the slab of wood starts to heat, though not enough yet to ignite. After several exhales, deliberately blowing at its base, new glints of orange-red flicker and emerge from the oxygen. They implore you to continue, urging you to help them turn the unburned timber ablaze. Stare too long, and they will acquiesce to the cold of the night. But should you coax these sparks, stoke and attend to them, they will consume the wood and burn bright.

Enkindled, it will warm you and illuminate the surrounding darkness with the reflection of your brilliant eyes. And it will continue to burn for you as long as you choose to care for

---

[78] I often write down things I see or hear that impact me. I recorded this while walking through the Pantheon in Rome.

it. Intensifying and gleaming on a grander stage, building the capacity to encompass more people than yourself. After some time, gratified by the heat and splendor of what you have built, you widen your view and see its larger significance. It once was merely you, alone with flickers of fire for company. But now stands a community, who warm themselves with and see through the light, which you created. Only now do you realize your importance.

Two parties appear on opposite ends of the spectrum in discourse over happiness. One is in a constant search for it; the other condemns it as meaningless. Both lines of thought have wandered off track. Living with pleasure as the sole aim is an error, but so is denouncing happiness as empty. Where these conclusions go awry is where we picture our states of mind, like joy, on our life's passage. Joy is *not* the promised land we search for, and it cannot be the X on our map. Instead, joy is the arc that carries us over the seas. Just as gratefulness is the wind that fills our sails and our desire to spend our time well is the accuracy of our compass. Or how love acts as the bedrock we finally build our homes on. This is not to say that other modes of being cannot get you where you need to go or support you, but I would argue that they might lead you astray. The uncalibrated compass is unpredictable, as are the fickle winds of the ungrateful, and the quicksand of dishonesty.

Joy, love, and confidence—these are not goals to accomplish. They are states of being. They are the way that we live our lives, not the end result. Do not search for love; live with love. Do not seek out joy; live joyfully. These conditions are here with you, now, waiting to be employed. But the birds sing to you, and you do not listen. The roses exude beauty for you, and you do not smell them. The sun rises for you, and you do not watch it. The light warms for you, and you do not feel it.

Every day of this journey is ours to take hold of and experience in whichever manner we desire. I might not be able to tell you where my adventure leads. Nor can I tell you if I will be happy or sad or angry at its end. But I am sure that I will leave this earth with love in my heart and joy on my lips. For those are the modes of being that I know to be best for interacting with, serving, and creating in the world.

Bread acts as the body of Christ, now understood worldwide as a symbol of sharing and generosity. Your works, your words, your drawings, your science, your circuits, your creations—these are the body of *you*. These are your way of expressing yourself to and interacting with your environment. Let that then be the basis for what you invent. Impact those around you—impact the world—by expressing yourself. Take the formulas and innovations of your mind and write them down in your own words. Give ideas inspired by others your own personal touch, if you are so bold.

It follows naturally that a necessary character trait of any prominent inventor is confidence. "Meek young men grow up in libraries, believing it their duty to accept the view which Cicero, which Locke, which Bacon, have given; forgetful that Cicero, Locke, and Bacon were only young men in libraries when they wrote these books."[79] It is your duty to understand those matters which have changed and currently change the world, but it is not your duty to accept them. To reject the status quo, however, takes courage. Imposters fail with original thought because they lack the assurance that their own ideas are worth listening to. At some point, you must find enough confidence to unveil *your* conclusions. You

[79] Ralph Waldo Emerson, "The American Scholar," *Essays* (New York: Charles E. Merrill & Co., 1907) para. 13.

must bring them forth in the face of criticism and adversity. You must risk failure and embarrassment.

Dr. Starzl was mocked by many peers while innovating with organ transplantation. Upon presenting at a conference the initial findings for his experiments in dogs, the results appeared bleak. One participant reproached him publicly and "asked wryly, if, rather than [perform] this complex operation, it might be easier to simply anesthetize the dog and have a laboratory assistant carry the animal from one table to another. The ripple of laughter from the audience completed [his] humiliation."[80] Yet, his willingness to endure criticism brought forth success. He succeeded not only because of his work ethic and creativity, but also through his confidence that there was a great potential for transplantation. His determination, among a couple other practitioners of the time, attracted innovators, university hospitals, and doctors from around the world. Inspired together, they made a massive and lasting impact on medicine as we know it.

This shows, in parallel, how our modes of being and personal expression help us manifest more than new technologies or arts. But by bringing forth and externalizing what you have stored in your mind, you also build yourself a new anchor point in the web of the world. Innovation has direct and indirect products. The direct being the surgery, the book, the bread. The indirect being the connection between surgeon and patient, between author and reader, between baker and consumer. Consequently, by building in the real world, we make it a more interconnected place. Keeping your ideas to yourself precludes their potential to make the world better. Doing this,

---

[80] Thomas E Starzl, *The Puzzle People: Memoirs of a Transplant Surgeon* (Pittsburgh: University of Pittsburgh Press, 2003), 78.

you remain a loose thread, one to be picked off in the wash. Choose, instead, to interact and invent and express. Help those around you by weaving your own personal stitch into this great tapestry that we call humanity.

Innovation has another intangible yet profound purpose. That is, it creates and provides hope. People thrive on hope, much like joy and love. This is a difficult result to comprehend because it is not quantifiable. We can try our best with brain imaging, psychology studies, and polls, but human feelings like hope are simply outside the scope of finding a true mechanism or explanation. This does not mean, however, that they are entirely imperceptible. You can see hope indirectly through a smile, an election ballot, or in a research grant. You can feel the effects of hope through a hug, from cold droplets of rain, or the warmth of the sun. Even if we do not experience it directly, it is an integral piece of our day-to-day lives. It is an inspiring reason for people to get out of bed in the morning, continue on with their work, or raise a family.

Medical research poses a good example. Stories from lives saved by new cures and procedures are not empirical. Tales of people whose vision or hearing or feeling may be returned (or created!) can only be retold and shared. Their true impact, outside of the person treated, cannot be measured. Everyone lives with the reality that they are mortal. People who do not are simply avoiding that inherent truth. "Life is short," right?

Constant innovation in the medical field plucks sensitive strings on the human conscience. We long to know that the diseases and traumas yet to befall us can be fixed and healed. Doctors and medical researchers are therefore symbols of hope to those who face eventual death—namely, everyone who is alive. This sentiment is not calculable nor tangible, but those conditions do not interfere with its bona fide reality.

Therefore, when you innovate, keep in mind that your actions and attitude do not only produce a physical result. Your creations—meaning your imagination when acted upon—provide hope. They become a potential inspiration to your bosses, your colleagues, your loved ones, your friends, and to yourself. If you need proof of this, you only need to look toward your heroes.

By asking myself who I want to be like in the future, I realized that there are many people who I admire. But the most concise list includes Steve Irwin, Warren Miller, and Indiana Jones. Those who know me will probably not find this surprising. It seems instinctive to pursue the path of your idols—though I admit that this is tough to do for a fictional character. However, I believe that there is a large difference between following in their footsteps and embodying your own actions which would make them proud of you. It is the fact that these men and women drew their own paths that inspires you. They were trailblazers, not followers. The greatest impact of this knowledge is the understanding that if what they did is possible, then you might be capable, too. *Your idols want you to be your own hero.*

It seems as if those who inspire us were put on this earth with an intention to change it. But this blends together two different concerns: the result of a life and the objective of a life. Just because you see a man's actions does not mean you understand the ambitions or ethos with which he took them. From here one might then ask, "What is a worthy objective, a worthy ambition, a worthy purpose for life?" I commonly hear the answer as something interchangeable with "to be fulfilled," or "to get the most out of each day." I believe these lead to a tale of wanting—waking up needy for something we're not sure of and going to sleep unsatisfied.

I would propose that such a purpose is to simply be our best selves. I feel for the spouse of a man who always needs more in life, for soon she will not be enough. But if instead her husband always desires to be a better person? That would lead him to try and be the best husband possible, not to want more from his marriage. Instead of *wanting more*, can we aspire to *be better*? Can that, in essence, be our sole purpose in life? Viktor Frankl's belief that "the true meaning of life is to be discovered in the world rather than within man or his own psyche,"[81] embodies the idea that we find meaning by interacting with the world. I propose we supplement this idea that purpose is found not just by interacting with the world, but rather by interacting *well* with the world in a way that would make you proud. Now, I'm not saying, "Don't focus on anyone besides yourself." Instead, my intention is this: Build your own character first, then see what good you can do in the world as that person.

I can imagine Steve Irwin, the famed Crocodile Hunter, waking up every day and thinking, even if subconsciously, "Today, I am going to work extremely hard, provide as much joy and excitement to the Australia Zoo visitors as possible, and be the greatest bloke I can be. Because by doing that, I will be able to help out the wildlife that I love so dearly. Crikey!" The reason he protected so much nature and created a massive influence was because he directed his focus toward being a good person. I believe this is the same foundational reason for most positive changes in the world.

On this topic of purpose, I've often heard people insist that they "just want to make an impact." And how hollow that rings. Without specific ambitions, they are empty words. Lack of a context to these assertions is what drives us toward anxiety on a quiet Sunday afternoon. "I want to be better!" means nothing without

---

[81] Viktor E. Frankl, Harold S. Kushner, and William J. Winslade, *Man's Search for Meaning* (Boston, MA: Beacon Press, 2014), 110.

following up with how or why. Furthermore, it's not about the absence of an answer to "What should I do?" but the absence of an answer to "Why should I do it?" Though I cannot be certain, your heroes most likely asked themselves this same question. And their response was to subdue their doubts through repeated, well-intentioned action. That pursuit of life is why you marvel at them.

Stop searching for impact. Spend that energy on doing what you believe needs to be done with the mindset you desire to have, now. I believe that it is in this state of being, regarding what is important in this moment, where you will find the handholds to lift yourself up. I believe that your prudent thoughts manifested in the physical world are what will provide hope and inspiration to those around you. I believe that when your personal expression meets bold action, purpose will find you.

THE WATER IS COLDER THAN I REMEMBER

Australia and Returning Home

March 4, 2020

I always offer surf lessons to people who are learning, pretty much no matter where I am. I think it's a fun way to get to know a person. Plus, I get to spend more time in the ocean, swimming around and bodysurfing. Win-win. Also, even though I always do it for free, the people I give lessons to usually buy me lunch. Win-win-win.

I made a Dutch friend in Byron Bay who wanted to learn, so I took her out this afternoon. The surf was trash from consistent north winds, but still good enough for pushing someone into little white water waves. Before going out, I remembered hearing about how the man-of-war jellyfish, known as bluebottles in Australia, floated on the surface and were mostly found in the northern waters. When the winds blow from the north, it brings with it some of the jellies. Having bodysurfed some small waves at the Byron Bay point the entire previous day without seeing—or feeling—one, I figured it was fine.

We went out and had a blast, and she caught a couple good waves. About an hour later, after her best wave yet, she fell off the board into shallow water. Standing up, she turned around with a super big smile. Then, in a flash, that stoke turned quickly to visceral pain and shock. *Whoops*. Rushing over to her I saw a handsome lookin' bluebottle, the body of which was about three-fourths the size of my palm. It was, in fact, a *really big* bluebottle. It stung her well across the inside of her right thigh, and then as I took the board from her and we got the stinger off, it stung her again on her opposite ankle. A real rippa! Getting her back to shore, we got it washed off, and it all was good. I mean, she was clearly in a lot of discomfort, but like, *I* didn't get stung, so … it's all good.

March 5, 2020

I met a pretty Uruguayan girl in the water in Byron Bay and asked her out for a drink. Neither of us had a phone at that moment, so we set a time at a random bar in town. While sitting at the bar, 20 minutes past the meeting time, figuring I'd been stood up, she cruised in. We had a beer and talked for an hour or two and really had a wonderful time. Similar interests, values, and all. Then she asked, "Do you want to go on an adventure?" Obviously, I said no. (I'm kidding. Of course I said yes.)

Thirty minutes later, she was driving us through a forest out of town. After a three-quarters-of-a-mile hike down through the trees, the light was starting to fade, and we walked out onto a gorgeous beach. Through all the commotion of trains and buses and hostels, I had never stopped to realize what I was missing in Australia. The coastline is far longer than that of the United States. If beaches like this were just a short drive out of town, imagine the adventures to be had way off the beaten path. Next time I come to Australia, I'm renting a car for sure.

March 7, 2020

If surfing Malibu is like driving around New York City on a normal day, then the Superbank in Coolangatta, QLD is like trying to drive through NYC at midnight on New Year's Eve. Not only is it crowded, it's crowded with wicked talented surfers. At most breaks, even if there's 20 people in the water, only four or five of them can actually surf. But here, every wave already has three guys on it, ripping up the face of it like a paper-shredder. Watching Snapper Rocks break while in the water is intimidating, let alone with the crowd of experienced surfers there. Make no mistake; no one is nodding you into a wave here. They are far more likely going to physically push you off of it.

March 16, 2020

I'm over hostels. I almost punched the guy next to me at 3 a.m. for his nonstop, bear-like snoring. From what I've experienced, hostels consist of two distinct factions. First there is a group that is simply traveling. Maybe their trip is a week long or a year long, but they fill their days with exploration and adventure. The second group is, for lack of better words, running away from life. On the surface, their days seem to be filled with fun, but quite quickly in conversation you realize there's an underlying depression. Working any job that would take them away from home, late nights and later mornings, spending all their remaining money on drugs and booze, and most of their conscious time focused on sex.

A couple experiences I've had so far epitomize this second group. The first was in Coffs Harbour, NSW. The night I stayed there was laid back, with only two dozen or so people in the entire hostel. Just a casual, rainy Tuesday, with nothing going on in the town, spent having a drink around the dinner table making some new friends. When I got up at 5:30 a.m. the next day to catch the bus, a group of three or four of them were still wide awake. Fairly nice and fun to talk to the night before, they were now skittish and wide-eyed. A couple still riding a high; the others starting to come down. With the sun not yet up, one yelled to me, "Ah mate! Bummer you went to sleep. We all got bored so we dropped MDMA and I had some extra for ya!" It's the thought that counts, right?

Another time, while in Noosa Heads, QLD, I was hanging out with a new friend at the bar of her hostel. They gave all the people staying there a ticket for "one hour of free drinks," which meant refills of a pink, kind-of sparkly cocktail they made. I'm all for a free drink, but I tried it and it tasted like someone dropped a vitamin C tablet into diluted Kool-Aid. Standing off to the side, talking with my friend, I watched the group of 20 or so people in line. When they got to the front, a girl would refill their cup from pitchers of a pre-batched cocktail she was regularly diluting with concentrated juice and sparkling water. Then, as they circled to the end of the line, they'd knock it back, always in a slow slog back toward the bar again. And they all did this for the entire hour. None of them were actually smiling, just sometimes chuckling apathetically at a joke or bobbing their head to the music. A bunch of listless teens and twenty-somethings, drifting through the night with a bloated stomach and a slight buzz—probably more from the sugar than the alcohol.

It reminds me of an experience I had in a gas station an hour or so outside of Dallas. It was a beautiful blue Texas Sunday afternoon in the middle of nowhere, on my way back from scuba diving in a rock quarry. At the quarry, there were a couple small planes and a 30-foot-long metal shark submerged 60 feet underwater that you could swim through ... sure, why not? Anyways, for some reason in Texas, Sundays are always nice. Even if there was a thunderstorm, tornado, or it was well below freezing for the entire week, it always cleared up for Sunday. In the middle of this wonderful bluebird day, these two guys sat lethargically in front of several slot machines tucked in the corner of the gas station, playing away their paychecks bit by bit. Quarter. Quarter. Pull. Music. Nothing. *Again.* Quarter. Quarter. Pull. Music. Nothing. *Am I happy now?* Quarter. Quarter. Pull. Music. Nothing. *Is it over yet?* Same with these young guys and girls in their prime in the hostel bar. Step. Step. Refill. Shoot it. Not drunk. *Again.* Step. Step. Refill. Shoot it. Not drunk. *Am I happy now?* Step. Step. Refill. Shoot it. Not drunk. *Is it over yet?*

March 19, 2020

In a matter of a week or two, the coronavirus pandemic fully took hold of the world's attention. Unfortunately, borders are shutting. I had been eyeing a ticket to South Africa, hoping to get to Jeffrey's Bay. Dreaming of celebrating my birthday in two weeks at the Cape of Good Hope. Finishing my trip by slowly backpacking through South America. I guess those experiences will have to wait for the future.

My last day in Noosa was nostalgic. The journey was ending abruptly to say the least. I said goodbye to several friends and gave away the surfboard I had bought. I watched a fantastic bright red sunset over the coast. A light weather system blew in from the south. Its brief shower filled the sky with a rainbow that sheltered Noosa Heads National Park. As I walked back to where I was staying next to Weyba Creek, complete darkness enveloped the day. I lit my path with the flashlight from my phone. Then, something flickered in the light, five feet or so in front of me at head-height. I shined my light upward and saw the back of a spider. It was the size of my hand, in the middle of the road, climbing up its web that had been blown out of the tree above. I had almost walked into it face first. Screw. That. All feelings of melancholy for leaving Australia quickly evaporated.

March 20, 2020

I had two goals while in Australia. One was to surf as many places as possible. The second was to see the Australia Zoo, which I was planning on doing later that week. However, the rapid onset of the coronavirus pandemic forced me to get out of the country before flights started getting cancelled. So, I got a bus from Noosa to Brisbane to fly back to Sydney for a flight home to San Francisco. Before my bus reached Brisbane, it stopped in Beerwah—at the Australia Zoo, of all places. I had to stay on the bus to catch my flight. I was *so close*—about 30 feet away—yet so far. I know that it will be there for a long time, and I plan on coming back. But, halfway around the world from home, driving into the parking lot, seeing the big images of Steve Irwin inviting me in, and not being able to get off the bus ... That was hard to swallow.

March 24, 2020

The water in San Francisco is colder than I remember. After getting back, I went out for a surf. Well, actually, I slept for a day, then I went out for a surf. There was still a bit of juice left in the North Pacific to be tasted before the springtime winds trashed the waves. The forecast was six to seven feet with light offshore winds. The Bay was welcoming me home.

While driving, I called a friend, and he told me that the surf was fun, "some 10-foot sets at Noriega," the street name across from where the wave he just surfed was breaking. *Ten foot?* Bringing only a 5'9" board might not have been my best call. To be fair, it paddles well, but still. At my skill level, I should be on a bit of a bigger board in that size surf. But I was already on Sunset Boulevard and wasn't going to turn around. I parked and watched for 30 minutes. The larger waves were fairly inconsistent. Smaller sets in the head high to slightly overhead range were more common. As I jumped in the water north of the Noriega sandbar, I realized that my 3/2mm wetsuit was nice and all, but a bit more neoprene would have been welcome ... three-plus months of surfing in board shorts made me soft. Right before reaching the outside, a huge set of waves started bumping up on the horizon. It built rapidly, convening on where I was paddling. Duck diving under the first wave, I had two thoughts in quick succession. First: *Jesus, that was big.* Second: *Fuck yeah, it is.*

Look, I don't claim to be a good surfer; hell, I don't even claim to be a surfer, really, but this was the largest I had ever surfed Ocean Beach here in San Francisco. This same beach had blown me to bits in past years with smaller waves than this. But now, in the cold water, paddling and bobbing over the blue-gray hills that rolled under an overcast sky, I was completely calm. Calm that I could safely handle myself in larger surf. Calm as I screamed across an overhead wall of water. Calm about being back home. And with this calmness of mind came excitement for what was to come. Excitement for the next waves which would peak over the horizon. For the work I would find and commit myself to. For the strong and intimate relationships I would build. For all the experiences that are headed my way.

Big storms are brewing far off in the distance, creating massive swells of life. They're going to bring me love and grief. Euphoria and disappointment. Success and failure. And I'm excited for all of it. *I'm excited for the adventure.*

What I must do is all that concerns me, not what the people think. This rule, equally arduous in actual and in intellectual life, may serve for the whole distinction between greatness and meanness. It is the harder, because you will always find those who think they know what is your duty better than you know it. It is easy in the world to live after the world's opinion; it is easy in solitude to live after our own; but the great man is he who in the midst of the crowd keeps with perfect sweetness the independence of solitude.

— Ralph Waldo Emerson, *Self-Reliance*

AUTHENTICITY

There is but a single path that I know,
Which exists only at the rise and fall.
Upon a glowing reflection accompanying her show,
A single line of light, viewed by all.

To witness it, one must only sit and watch,
Hear the warblers whistle and the winds whisper,
And gaze upon the waves that wash.

But travel this path no one may,
For its ephemeral beauty will never last.
To her I promise I'll live another day,
Until the sun to me has sent its cast. [82]

— "A Radiant River"

Sitting boldly at the apex of the value hierarchy, its worth built on originality and sincerity, is the independent conductor of all other values. It is the most important to act out in its entirety, yet the most difficult. For each independent value has its own impediments. And the composite of all their obstacles constitutes the immense barrier blocking honest self-expression. There is but a small group of men that we recognize

---

[82] I wrote this while sitting on a bench, facing west over White Rock Lake in Dallas, TX.

to have surmounted these hurdles. And though we do not understand exactly what they possess, we know it to be attractive and true. When we see genuine expression written in ink, we call it poetry. When we see genuine expression written in action, we call it authenticity.

With each passing year, people are becoming more interconnected. Because of this, the authority of our own values is being challenged with a far greater strength than ever before in history. In order to be one's self a hundred years ago, a man would have had to reject the influence of thousands. Now, he must reject the influence of millions. Each day is fraught with images and videos of the ostensible success of others from around the entire globe. More self-doubt than you could ever handle is vibrating every thirty seconds in your pocket, and we, as a whole, are too weak to resist its control.

Likewise, it is not just the influence of others, but also the ability for modern technology to rapidly project our actions worldwide. The youth of today grow up in a manner that has never been seen. Our judicial system may be able to confine one within a concrete cell, but it is the masses of this world which might forever detain us in our own minds. Bounded by no walls, we are instead imprisoned by the thoughts of others. And for understandable reason. The immature action of an adolescent can, if propelled into the spotlight by the right people, ruin his or her image in a moment's notice. Broadcast to the world by those who have forgotten that humanity is full of confusions and blunders, especially at a young age. Even if well-intentioned, this creates an intimidating environment. It is difficult enough to be yourself when you are surrounded by the deceptive veneer of success. But when this climate is augmented with the fear of being besieged by what appears to be the entire world, genuineness might seem unthinkable. And make no mistake, this is the world we live in.

Maybe the heroes of yesterday were celebrated for their work with swords, guns, or legislation, for those were the boldest actions known at the time. But the heroes of today will emerge because of their ability to act authentically. We live in a world that attempts to teach morality from a book instead of from the heart and pre-determines mistakes as evils to be avoided. It is in this world that these heroic men and women will remind us of the beautiful fact that we are human. They will brandish the armor of their values and hold their heads up boldly. They will show us what is precious in life. And we will exalt them for exactly that.

Where this value search must start is with nature's most primordial gift to humankind: our most basic, primal emotions. That I can be joyous, that I can be angry, that I can be sad. These are, at the most fundamental level, one of our greatest connections to nature. They are experiences everyone can appreciate, if they are willing, for there are no external barriers preventing them from doing so. When it is time for joy, the authentic man will shout toward the sky. But behold! When it is time for tears, he will also cry.

The eminent photographer of the Sierra, Ansel Adams, believed that because photography requires genuine expression with regard to what is being captured, each photograph inherently delineates part of what that person experiences with the world itself.[83] So, too, does our involvement with and interpretation of life as a whole come from each interaction with emotion. Every snapshot of affection or empathy or despair is integral to the way each of us understands life.

---

[83] Ansel Adams, "A Personal Credo," *The American Annual of Photography 1944, Volume Fifty-Eight* (Boston: American Photographic Publishing Co.; London: Chapman and Hall, LTD., 1943). I recommend searching for and reading the small excerpt this sentiment comes from, because it is a delightfully eloquent and insightful passage.

How could a man ever know if something is immoral or inauthentic if he has silenced his own emotional response to it? That deep, jagged feeling in your gut, the lightness in your chest, or the relief of pressure from your shoulders and forehead. These are the signs that you feel what you see to be right or wrong or good or evil. Will you listen to them?

This subject has an immense collection of scientific (and pseudoscientific) literature, which I find to be of little consequence. For centuries, man has tried to categorize emotions and feelings, naming them and attempting to find out their purpose. However, even if similar from person to person, their actual existence in each (i.e. the independent emotional experience of every man) is unique. It is unnecessary to fixate so strongly upon their cataloging in order to appreciate them.

In some areas of life, the more you attempt to define it, the less you are able to live in and experience it. In essence, all that matters is that you *embrace* this gift from nature. The gift of feeling. Show me who you are by showing me how you feel. Bare everything— your wonder, your delight, your contentment, your calm, your anguish, and your heartache. Expose it, appreciate it, and you will understand it without any need to define it.

Awareness of your primal emotions is only the first step. It is but a provocation for *action*. I believe that those who lead their lives by consistent, well-aimed actions are ubiquitous in the world of excellence. This theme is pervasive in celebrated literature. It is in Athena's words to Telemachus that his future will be proud, "if in [him] stirs the brave soul of [his] father, and [he] like [his father] can give effect to *word and deed*."[84] Odysseus,

---

[84] Homer, *The Odyssey of Homer,* translated by George Herbert Palmer (Boston and New York: Houghton, Mifflin and Company, 1891), 23. My italics and rearrangement of the words "deed" and "word."

Telemachus' father, was the embodiment of a Homeric hero and the recipient of most of the Greek gods' support because of his character. He spoke of and pursued his goals consistently and judiciously. The action-oriented life is found, too, in the Buddhist remembrances, ideas to be meditated on regularly. "I am the owner of my deeds and heir to my deeds. Deeds are my womb, my relative and my refuge. I shall be the heir of whatever deeds I do, whether good or bad."[85] Here we come to understand that each and every aspect of our life is *born from* and *reliant on* our deeds. Further, it is found in the transcendentalist movement in a John Fletcher quote as restated by Emerson: "Our acts our angels are, or good or ill,/ Our fatal shadows that walk by us still."[86] That we might see our future as entirely dependent on how we choose to act *now*. Even heavenly intervention would pale in comparison to our own positive decisions.

And yet, we do not live with these words in the forefront of our minds. We do not act as we intend to for a variety of reasons. One reason I know, which reverberates more deeply in our psyches than many others, is insecurity. The self-conscious acquiesce to their surroundings. While hoping it will abate their unease, all it does is lead to a perpetual state of mental discord. This is that woeful condition where we feel in real time how disconnected our actions are from our intentions. And how unfortunate it is that so many men will act poorly because of how they think others might perceive them. On this theme, I have always appreciated the cliché: "When a man turns 20, he cares greatly about what others

---

[85] *Numbered Discourses: A Translation of the Aṅguttara Nikāya*, Translated by Bhikkhu Sujato (SuttaCentral, 2018) https://suttacentral.net/an5.57/en/sujato, Numbered Discourses 5, Dutiyapaṇṇāsaka, Hindrances, Subjects for Regular Reviewing, para. 6.
[86] Ralph Waldo Emerson, "Self-Reliance," in *Essays: First Series.* (Boston: J. Munroe and Company, 1847), 37. From Epilogue to Beaumont and Fletcher's Honest Man's Fortune.

think of him. When he turns 40, he stops caring about what those people might think. And when he turns 60, he realizes no one was thinking about him in the first place." Realize that the only person who will judge you by the sum of all your actions, for better or for worse, is you.

Anxiety and apprehension over the thoughts of others can only be overtaken by the understanding of their result. Succumbing to self-conscious thoughts will lead to stagnation and deeds that don't reflect who you wish to be. The most compelling commentary I have found, which speaks bluntly to the conclusion of poor action, is the Bhagavad-Gita: "Those untaught, / And those without full faith, / and those who fear," will find "No peace ..., / no hope, nor happiness," here in this world or anywhere else.[87] I find the legitimacy of these words in my unease upon reading them. The ignorant, the faithless, and the fearful squander their lives. Their character embodies inaction and their efforts are hollow. Their words lack weight, and their lives grow dull. All because they choose not to stand up for themselves and what they believe.

Well worn over this theme is the saying, "Actions speak louder than words." This is, at heart, an argument in the debate of what a man does versus who a man is. There are those who believe themselves to embody certain values and ways of life. Their minds convince them that they are a "type" of person. Examples include: "I am honest" or "I am responsible." I find that there is little value in these statements and that they hurt more than they help. These words create an identity with which you will then associate yourself in the future.

---

[87] Vyasa, *The Song Celestial. or Bhagavad-Gita (From the Mahabharata)* (New York: Truslove, Hanson & Comba, Ltd., 1900), Chapter IV, lines 143-146.

Though we will love this confident image of ourselves, "There is no permanent wise man ... We have been ourselves that coward ... and shall be again, not in the low circumstance, but in comparison with the grandeurs possible to the soul."[88] We are human; we make mistakes and act in ways that we don't believe live up to our morals. When this happens, if we have created a concrete image of who we are, these inconsistent or conflicting actions will bring with them anguish and self-doubt. Furthermore, they might lead us to create multiple identities, each based on our current environment—such as acting one way at work, one way at home, and one way with our friends. And so our lives become shows for others, imitating a false figure instead of being our true selves.

Free yourself from these shackles. Without the restraint of inflexible identities, you can appreciate all of your actions as your own, instead of pushing away those that you do not like. This is to wake up each morning with the thought, "I am not honest, nor am I dishonest, but today will give myself plenty of opportunities to act honestly." It is in today that we live; it is in today that we show who we are. And it may be intimidating to maintain this constant level of accountability. But if you do, you create the freedom to contradict previous behavior without attacking yourself for doing so. You kindly open up the opportunity to compare what you want your actions to say about you to what they *actually* say about you. This is a wonderful state for growth because it supports your capacity to learn from mistakes.

Further growth is stimulated by those who band around you. If you wish to be surrounded by people you admire, you must take responsibility for your actions. Those who refuse to do so affix

---

[88] Ralph Waldo Emerson, "Spiritual Laws," in *Essays: First Series* (Boston: J. Munroe and Company, 1847), 124.

themselves as insignificant to society. "Common men are apologies for men; they bow the head, excuse themselves with prolix reasons, and accumulate appearances because the substance is not."[89] Any method of masking or avoiding your truth hinders you because all of your deeds are the proclamation of your values to your peers. There is no hiding from this truth: Your actions define your visible value system. The men and women with whom you wish to congregate are constantly fleeing from people with poor value systems and flocking to those with good ones.

Furthermore, prioritizing individual action over a permanent identity serves to place equal importance on all of your deeds. This holds true for future decisions that have yet to be made. Everything you might do becomes an opportunity to show yourself, and others, what is important to you. Every action turns into a demonstration of honesty or responsibility or love. More tangible than this, however, is the output of your actions. All men have the potential to deliver great wonder, just as they can great wickedness. When you act well, you prevent the potential corruption in you from escaping. You preclude that option by bringing good into the world.

It must be stated that people are both enraged and emboldened by such authenticity, regardless of your good intentions. Taking your own stance will always draw dissent and ridicule from some. Yet for each man you displease with your actions, you will encourage a dozen others. Even if they disagree with your beliefs, your honest action will hearten their desire to speak and act for themselves, too.

Consequently, it should then be the priority to leave your focus solely on your actions. Acting well, in accordance with your

---

[89] Ralph Waldo Emerson, "Spiritual Laws," in *Essays: First Series* (Boston: J. Munroe and Company, 1847), 144

values and best intentions, obviates any need to speak of or believe in a concrete version of yourself. That information will instead be signed brazenly into the firmament by the light in your eyes.

I fear, though, that I digress too far toward theory. To the philosophy of great women and men and not to great women and men themselves. It is indisputable that having people in your life who you admire is important. Through our emotional response to their actions, this select group teaches us about respect. They continue a lineage of distinction. Their ancestors consist of an independent soul that connects them not by blood but by honor. You might find them in your companions, in your literature, or in your forebears.

Two figures take particular notice in emboldening my actions. Even though I was born without meeting either of my grandfathers, I have long cherished the privilege to hear stories and memories from those who lived with them. Both were great men in different spheres of the world. One a pilot whose career started because he, in his own words, "felt a strong duty to serve [his] country and *wanted* to go into service, *especially* after Pearl Harbor was attacked."[90] The other an engineer who, through a lifetime of dedicated work, became a respected leader for many. There is no need to disclose more detail of their lives; simply put, they were good, courageous people. I have an innate respect for them through the tales of their proud actions.

Their stories introduced me to a truth: Boldness is in my blood. It is in both of my strong and independent parents. It is in my grandfathers that worked and served communities around the world. It is in my grandmothers who raised and led strong families. It is in my ancestors who raised livestock in California and

---

[90] Taken from my grandfather's unpublished autobiography. My own italics.

in their predecessors who traveled on faith via the Mayflower to America. It is in some of those whose legacy has been lost to time, whose brave adventures I will never hear. But I declare this not just for myself. *Boldness is in all our blood.* In each of our ancestors there are a select few who carried this authentic torch, and in *all* of their descendents there is the spark to propagate its flame.

Respect is that attitude and weight we associate with a man's words and actions. It is the heavy calm of my mind that occurs when I listen to those who I admire, as I do with the stories of my grandfathers. I subconsciously filter through the noise of the masses for the words of these people because of the force behind them. The words of Thoreau resonate here, that "the virtues of a superior man are like the wind, the virtues of a common man are like the grass; the grass, when the wind passes over it, bends."[91] My attention gravitates toward those that I respect because I feel that I have more to learn from them than others.

Acting as the foundation of solid families and friendships, respect helps to build the wonders of the world. Two people who respect each other have each decided independently that their counterpart's words deserve to be listened to and analyzed. That their actions deserve to be seen, and that their intentions, even if misguided, are good. It takes time to get to this place because respect can only be earned, never requested. It is not received through fear, through guilt, nor through any other action which aims to acquire it. Men receive this gift of respect from others solely because of their internal desire to act honorably.

This idea applies not only to others, but to ourselves as well. Self-respect is the magnitude of worth that we place on our own

---

[91] Henry David Thoreau, *Walden, Or, Life in the Woods* (Boston and New York: Houghton, Mifflin, & Company, 1906), 191.

beliefs, actions, and desires. I believe that this is tougher to gain than respect from others. For each man knows the full gamut of poor actions that he has taken. A man respects himself when he lives well and acts with dignity now, not for immediate reward, but because he knows that it is the only way he should live at the moment. Only *after* he took bold action, only *after* he spoke his truths, only *after* he accomplished good deeds, did others investigate why or how he did what he did.

> *The great man knew not that he was great. It took a century or two for that fact to appear. What he did, he did because he must; it was the most natural thing in the world, and grew out of the circumstances of the moment. But now, every thing he did, even to the lifting of his finger or the eating of bread, looks large, all-related, and is called an institution.*[92]

If you wish for respect, for honor, for greatness, do not look elsewhere—look within yourself. Look at the reasons why you would give yourself respect. Only once you admire yourself will others consider the idea of doing the same.

Authenticity is the consolidation of all that you believe to be important exhibited in your actions. It is the present state of being, where you act as yourself because that is the only person you genuinely know how to be. By attempting to use another person's image, you throw away your potential. Instead, bring out your truth. Live perpetually as yourself so that you might say at the end of your day, "They would not find me changed from

---

[92] Ralph Waldo Emerson, "Spiritual Laws." Essay. In *Essays: First Series* (Boston: J. Munroe and Company, 1847), 139.

him they knew—/Only more sure of all I thought was true."[93] These words of Robert Frost do not attend exclusively to the reflection of others, but also to the inherent truth that how you act right now decides your future. "Character is fate."[94] It is in a man's best interest to portray his values in all his actions because that is what will lead to his most prosperous possible life.

He spends his time well so that he might create a lifelong adventure. He gets rid of the needless clutter that weighs him down. He takes strong, calm breaths; loves those dear to him with all his heart; and speaks forthrightly. He reveres the world and all its wonder for the authentic experiences it has to offer. He lifts his posture up against the gravity of humanity, demanding accountability for all his actions and words, regardless of the situation. He expresses his thoughts, intending to interlace them with reality. And when he falls short of these actions—as he inevitably will—he gets back up and tries again.

In moments of joy brought on by a passed test, by a promotion at work, by a passionate kiss, or by a well-ridden wave, he indulges in the accomplishment. His mind murmurs to him that maybe, because of this successful effort, this good fortune, he can let up a bit on his values. To this, he responds to his mind, knowing of the impermanence of such events, and says, "Do not believe it. Nothing can bring you peace but yourself. Nothing can bring you peace but the triumph of principles."[95]

And with that it comes to a close, this journey of virtue. It begins and concludes with a question, as it always does.

---

[93] Robert Frost, "Into My Own." A Boy's Will (New York: Henry Holt and Company, 1915), lines 13-14.
[94] This saying is often credited to Heraclitus, a Greek philosopher.
[95] Ralph Waldo Emerson, "Self-Reliance," in *Essays: First Series*. (Boston: J. Munroe and Company, 1847), 79.

How will you live today? Imagine that you stand upon the coast, watching the ephemeral orange inferno dance above the horizon. Casting its last great aurora of the day over the world; stretching one sublime branch of light out across the water toward you. Where this radiant river ends in front of your feet, the parched sand begins, thirsting for the rise of the tides. Your hands reach down together, maybe in curiosity, maybe in subconscious worship. You grasp at the earth, picking up a great mound of the beige-white sand. But it's slipping through your hands. The weather-battered grains pouring away, a cataract of seconds in time. Quick, you must act before they are all gone. Before your life settles on the earth in the darkness and is washed back into the sea. Close this book; you don't need it. You never did. You know who you are and what is important in your life—what your values are. Now, before the time is out. Be someone you will be proud of.

See consciously. Think critically. Act accordingly.

Experience. Speak. Move.

Go.

Sincerely Stoked,

Flint Mitchell

NOTE FROM THE AUTHOR

My editors convinced me that the following sentiment, as it was originally written, wasn't the warmest of introductions, so I think this is a good place for it:

You shouldn't be reading this book.

Now, what I mean by that is that I never intended to show anyone these essays. They were my own personal 25th birthday present—to declare to myself what I believed to be important in life so that I could reflect on them and reorient when I needed to in the future. Each essay was supposed to be a page. It wasn't supposed to be a book. But then I blinked, and there it was.

I gave the book to some beta readers with instructions to effectively snuff me out. I told them, "Be as honest and critical as you can. Tell me *every* reason you do not like this book." I was proud of the work at that point, and I didn't need approval of its quality for personal use. However, I did need to know that I tried my best with it, and that included knowing if it could provide value to others. I eagerly awaited the feedback, rubbing my hands together in anticipation of the welcomed rejection so that I could move on with my life. Instead, one of the beta readers told me, "I don't say this lightly: *This book positively changed my life*. These essays are amazing, and they're something I think more people should read.

I truly believe that I should be the one paying YOU for letting me read them." And then he returned my money. *Who does that!?* I read his review a couple of times, then stared out of the window in front of me into a blue sky on a calm day in the middle of the pandemic, realizing this was only the beginning.

That feedback scared the shit out of me because of how personal this work is. If you criticize parts of this book, you are inherently criticizing parts of my own character (or at least my character aspirations), something I don't take lightly. And that's okay! If you disagree with me, that's rad! I can handle criticism; it's how I grow. Everything I say is open for discourse. I even consider starting discourse related to these topics to be a major success. At the same time, opening up to that possibility with this level of vulnerability is *terrifying*.

My biggest fear with this type of writing is the possibility that you might think I am preaching to you. As I said earlier, I wrote this *for me*. Because it's one thing to look at yourself in the mirror and say, "I don't like how I look right now; I should lose some weight." It's a *whole other thing* to tell someone else to look in the mirror—which is not my intent. If you felt like I've preached to you on how you should live your life, then I've failed in that sense. I hope I didn't.

I don't have a degree in philosophy, but I like reading it. I'm not that great at surfing, but I love doing it. I haven't invented the cure to cancer, but damn, wouldn't it be swell if I did? What I'm trying to say is that I'm not some embodiment of success and virtue—far from it. I'm just a guy. A guy who does things, some well, some decently, some poorly. But I always strive to do those things that would make me proud and to do them as best as I can. To re-quote Emerson, "The only gift is a portion of thyself. Thou must bleed for me."[96] This book is as close as I can get to giving a portion of myself to you. These words are, in essence, my blood. I put all I had into it over the past couple years and I'm damn proud of it. I enjoyed writing it, and I hope you enjoyed reading it.

If you've made it this far, let me know! I'd love to hear your thoughts, so message me at seekingauthenticitybook@gmail.com. I'll try to respond if you do. If you're interested in further information about this book or my podcast (also called *Seeking Authenticity*), check out my website, flintmitchell.com. Lastly, if you share this book with a friend or family member who you think would like it, that would help give this writing visibility! Thanks!

---

[96] Ralph Waldo Emerson, "Gifts," *Essays: Second Series* (Boston: James Munroe and Company, 1844), 175.

ACKNOWLEDGMENTS

As I mention in the note from the author, when I finished this book, no one had read more than some minor bits and pieces of it. By and large, it was entirely untouched by eyes other than my own, and I was happy with it. Regardless of what happens now, whether it becomes a best seller or only my mom and I read it (Hi mom!), I'm so glad I ended up sharing it. The people who read, commented on, questioned, analyzed, edited, reviewed, challenged, laughed with (or laughed at) this book helped me question its content, and therefore helped me question myself. I won't be able to remember everyone who helped influence this work, but for someone asking for "gratefulness" as a fixed epithet, I certainly have to try.

First and foremost I would like to acknowledge the unbelievable privileges that were granted to me in this life by my family. The opportunities I have been blessed with so far are nothing short of a miracle, and I am in awe of them everyday. I can't count the moments where a sunset, a bird's song, or the glare of light passing through desert dust stopped me in my tracks and forced me to question if it's all real—if I really got *this* lucky.

That sentiment goes for my mom and dad but also for my larger family and the generations that preceded them. Mom and dad: You helped teach me how to be responsible, how to question the world, and how to strive to be better. But you also helped me learn how to adventure, how to have fun, and how to prioritize personal expression. To my brother Alden: Your drive to fix problems in the world is inspiring (and intimidating sometimes). To my grandmothers: Dawn, I've said it before and I'll say it again: you're a badass. Some of my dry humor must come from you. Lisa, we miss you. I wish we could help you pick apricots from the trees in your backyard and bake pretzels and pancakes with you again. To my uncle Robert: You're a great uncle, and I hope you continue to look forward and point out the positive aspects of life! To my grandfathers: I can only hope to replicate your stories in my own way. Ralph, stories of you remind me to find love and adventure in life. Alden, stories of you remind me to focus and work hard.

My editors, Lori Lynn and Clare Fernández. Mental growth is tough to identify or measure. When I look back on the manuscript that I sent you at the beginning, I can physically see how I have changed. I asked that part of this editing process help me grow as a writer, and you delivered. I'm glad that you weren't phased by the level of attention I planned to spend on this book—quite the opposite in fact. The energy you invested into this work is tangible. I am so grateful for your edits, questions, and insight. You helped me create something that I will proudly pass on to my own eventual family.

Roommates and friends who visited or travelled with me along the way and entertained my sometimes relentless existential inquiry: Cheesesteak, thanks for letting me bounce ideas off you in our blue hut on the North Shore. Alex Arentsen, my bad for accidentally sandbagging you with an overhead high-tide session at Jack's right after you asked me to be your best man! Girth House owner Matt Montsinger, you phoned me after we hadn't talked for a couple years while I was sitting in a bar in Ventura reading

Friendship by Emerson. Couldn't be a coincidence, because two months later we were diving with each other next to sea turtles. Matt Leanse, you're sharper than all the fine kitchen knives you keep saying you won't buy more of. Susanne Kooij, thanks for your honest perspective with this book. The next surf lesson won't include any jellyfish, promise! Madison McKay, thanks for being a good friend, a positive light, and for helping me develop ideas about life during and after university. Donovan McGibben, I've got you 3 of 5 in our next chess series. DJ BKAYE, thanks for letting me crash with you in LA and for spurring me on to buy that ticket to Australia. Spenis and Adumb, are you doctors yet?

The families and people who provided couches, beds, or floors to sleep on or driveways to park in: The Arentsen family, I am always available to crash your Hawaiian vacations! My godmother Kerin, your love and generosity is limitless. The Harbisons, I am so grateful for your hospitality on Oahu! Gary Silberstein, thanks for the surf sessions, place to park, and introductions in Santa Cruz. Gary M., thanks for letting me stay in your driveway for a couple weeks. Tom Kaheli, thanks for the spot to park and pick up soccer in Ventura. Karen M. and Todd F., that was the best house-sitting gig ever! The Wolnys, thank you for letting me stay with you in San Luis Obispo and for the introduction to Toni Morrison. The Walkers, thanks for your generosity in Seattle. The Spurlocks and Melbyes, thanks for letting me stay in your place in San Diego. To the Waidyatillekas, howzit!!

Ellen Leanse, thank you for sharing what you've learned as an author with me and for reading and reviewing this work! I am so grateful for your time.

All those who read segments of this book and provided feedback and support: Miles Weiss, Nikki Wolny, Scott Fleishman,

Richard Miller, Martin Spencer, Gabby Zanutta, Randy Davis, and Max Pantalena.

The mentors, coaches, teachers, and professors who took care of, supported, inspired, taught, and coached me: Mike Graczyk, Kris Quintana, Barbara Varenhorst, Mark and Cheryl Goodman-Morris, Lisa Otsuka, Mike Amoroso, Mike Tillson, Cindy White, Julie Brody, Ashley Pogue, Rian Jorgensen, Michelle Mazzei, Karen Clancy, Barbara Cottrell, Jacob Pickard, Greg Markoulakis, Gregg Olson, Juraj Topolancik, Carlos Davila, Simon and Victor Ireland, Aman Kebreab, and Peter Weber.

Warren and Laurie Miller for responding to my letter.

That couple on Cascade Head near Lincoln City who helped plant the seed for this book in my mind on that beautiful, sunny hike.

Kristen Esquivias and Stacy McGinty, for asking questions that required me to reassess what I valued.

The guard at Kelly Slater's wave pool for not letting me in. I'm sure I'll be getting an invite from Kelly himself in the mail anytime now!

My longest hospice patient when I was a volunteer: they told you up to six weeks and you decided on two years. That's the spirit I'm talking about!

If I haven't mentioned your name, I guess you don't matter. Kidding, of course—there are many more people that have probably influenced this work or my travels but that I can't quite pin exactly how. I am grateful for all of you as well.

ABOUT THE AUTHOR

Flint Mitchell is a young research scientist and outdoorsman from the Bay Area, California. He has a degree in electrical engineering from Southern Methodist University, a couple of published patents, and a podcast (also named *Seeking Authenticity*). Flint is a self-proclaimed expert of several things: overanalyzing the minutia of the natural world around him, watching sunsets, and smiling. In his free time, you'll find Flint paddling in the ocean, reading a book, hiking his way out of cell service, or sitting next to a grill.

Made in the USA
Columbia, SC
28 December 2021

52891971R00126